Teaching Beginning Writing

Written by
Jo Fitzpatrick

Editor: Karen P. Hall
Illustrator: Ann Iosa
Project Director: Carolea Williams

Table of Contents

Letter from the Author   4

Introduction   5

Developmental Stages
  of Beginning Writing   6

Teaching Beginning Writers   9

Teaching Tips   10

Writing and Spelling   11

Handling Handwriting   13

Helping ESL Students   14

Record-Keeping and Assessment   15

Parent Involvement   15

Activities

Stage 1: Pre-Emergent Writers

Story Log   19

Do It Yourself   20

Backward Stories   21

Line 'Em Up   22

Cut and Tell   23

In the Beginning   24

Mix and Match   25

Story Detectives   26

Highlighter's Delight   27

Secretary Pool   28

Stage 2: Emergent Writers

Build a Sentence   29

Half Sentences   30

Pop-Up Sentences   31

Pull-Through Sentences   32

Creating Captions   33

Color-Coded Sentences   34

Match 'Em Up   35

Scrambled Sentences   36

Flip-Open Fun   37

Switcheroo   38

Stage 3: Early Writers

Imagination Time   39
Who Did What Where?   40
Super Pop-Ups   41
Stand-Up Sentences   42
Sentence Show   43
More Scrambled Sentences   44
Lights, Camera, Action!   45
Cinquains, Anyone?   46
Questions and Answers   47
Meet Mr. Story Face   48

Stage 4: Developing Writers

Story Swap   49
It's All in the Picture   50
Elastic Sentences   51
Peek-a-Boo Stories   52
Connect a Story   53
Read My Mind   54
Sentence Builders   55
Story Ladders   56
Story Walk   57
Story Stumpers   58

Stage 5: Established Writers

Story Outlines   59
Sentence Starters   60
Dinosaur Details   61
Digging for Details   62
Super Story Walk   63
Oh, P-L-E-A-S-E!   64
Story Snake   65
He Said, She Said   66
What Did You Say?   67
Think It Through   68

Reproducibles and Resources   69

Letter from the Author

Dear Readers,

Having taught for nearly 30 years, I have witnessed every phase of frustration with writing, from tears and tantrums to total disillusionment—and that reaction was from the teachers! I courted language experiences, cloze and pattern stories, creative-writing smorgasbords, whole-language themes, and writer's workshops. However, there was one "little" problem that remained unresolved . . . the students still couldn't write.

The solution dawned on me when my first child entered the teenage years: budding writers, like teenagers, need ample structure and guidelines *before* they are given too much freedom. I was motivating my young writers, challenging them, providing them with all the necessary tools, and setting them free to write *without* giving them the know-how to do so. In other words, they needed to be taught how to develop their thinking before they communicate and how to actually express their thoughts into words and sentences.

Thus began the crusade to give my "writing warriors" the "how-to" along with the "what to." Once my students understood the specific structure and format of a writing activity, they were better able to write independently, progressing beyond oral expression into sentence formation and eventually story development. Not only was the approach easy to implement and teach, my students were learning how to write well-structured and meaningful stories.

This resource book includes the writing principles and practices that have been proven successful, not only with my students, but with those of my colleagues. I hope that you and your students find the activities and guidelines just as motivating and rewarding, using them as a springboard for success in the dynamic world of writing.

Jo Fitzpatrick

Jo Fitzpatrick

Introduction

Children are born with the innate desire to communicate. In the early years, they label, mimic, experiment with spoken sentences, and engage in "verbal play." As they develop and grow, there is a natural tendency for children to expand their love of language into written expression; first through random scribbles and symbols, and then with specific words and sentences.

Successful writing requires four key elements: the desire to say something, the vocabulary to say it, the structure with which to write it, and the ability to make words. Current efforts to teach writing through the use of the "writing process," writing workshops, journal writing, and individual writing conferences may prove effective for students already exposed to structured writing, but these methods can be highly frustrating for young students still struggling with the simple task of getting their writing to make sense.

Teaching Beginning Writing is a complete writing resource that offers stimulating activities and numerous reproducibles to help teachers capitalize on children's natural love of language. The lessons provide clear, structured guidelines to help young writers clarify their ideas, maintain focus, and connect their thoughts to form related words and sentences. The writing program described in this book progresses through five sequential writing stages that specifically address the needs of beginning writers. The activities are generic and flexible in nature to accommodate different ability levels, to allow for homogeneous or heterogeneous grouping, and to fit easily into current classroom curriculum. Each skill is introduced at the oral level so students can readily formulate their ideas before trying to write them on paper. Graphic organizers, picture prompts, and sentence starters are also provided to help students express their thoughts verbally and in writing.

The overall goal of this writing program is to assist students in becoming thoughtful, self-improving writers. Once young children know how to write a good, "element-rich" sentence, they can easily expand those elements into a story. Through adequate exposure, engagement, and experience, students will be able to organize what they want to say, discover the vocabulary with which to say it, use structure in writing it, and strengthen their ability to make words. In other words, they will learn the "how-to" of writing.

Developmental Stages of Beginning Writing

Learning to write is a monumental task for both the student and the teacher. It involves more than simply "putting talk down on paper." It is an ongoing process that is dependent on a child's maturation, exposure, and experience. To best support and encourage beginning writers, teachers should be aware of the developmental stages of writing, adjust instruction to meet the needs and abilities of individual students, and incorporate other aspects of language development into the writing process.

Beginning writers progress through a continuum of skills and abilities, acquiring "building blocks" to help them advance and excel to the next level of learning. This resource book groups these skills and abilities into five different developmental stages. Use the following writing sequence to identify and assess the writing capabilities of your students. Keep in mind that students may not consistently move forward in their progress or finish one stage before moving on to the next.

Stage 1: Pre-Emergent Writer

- Has little or no understanding of the alphabetic principle—using specific letters to represent sounds. "Writing" consists of scribbles, random symbols, and strings of unrelated letters.
- Has an overall understanding of story content and structure.
- Dictates sentences and stories, including rewrites of literature, sentences for pictures, and stories based on personal experiences.
- Begins to develop *phonemic awareness*—the ability to hear, identify, and manipulate sounds in spoken language. Can write some letters, but still reverses them on occasion.
- Progresses into letter/sound correspondence and word writing. Gets a better sense of beginning and ending letters as well as spacing between words. Uses invented spelling, and can write some "sight words" (e.g., *the, me, like*) from visual memory.

Stage 2: Emergent Writer

- Forms new words by recombining *phonemes* or sound units (for example, *bat* to *cat*). On occasion, may reverse letter order within words.
- Identifies sentence components and word functions. Writes words or phrases to complete *patterned sentences*—sentences that have the same beginning or ending (for example, *I see a <u>man</u>* and *I see a <u>cat</u>*).
- Begins to write simple, unrelated sentences that include some punctuation. Uses literature as a model to compose nonpatterned sentences that express ideas and opinions.

Stage 3: Early Writer

- Expands sentences to express more complete thoughts.
- Combines and organizes simple, related sentences to form a short paragraph.
- Uses consistent invented-spelling patterns.
- Begins to write three-part stories that include a character, a setting, and an action (e.g., stories that describe "who," "doing what," and "where"). The stories are usually descriptive or narrative.

I go to the park with my friend.
We play. I like the park.

Stage 4: Developing Writer

- Expands three-part stories into five-part stories that include a character, a setting, an action, a time sequence, and a personal response (e.g., stories that describe "who," "doing what," "where," "when," and "why").
- Uses standard spelling with greater frequency, especially words with silent letters, *r*-controlled vowels, and homonyms.
- Punctuates sentences on occasion, but not consistently.
- Describes story parts with greater detail.
- Begins to experiment with different writing styles, including informational writing, descriptive stories, and simple narratives.

I like to play in the park with my friend. We play games and fly kites. We throw a ball to my dog Shaggy. We have lots of fun.

Stage 5: Established Writer

- Composes stories that have a clear beginning, middle, and end.
- Includes a distinctive "voice" when writing stories. Has a good sense of "audience."
- Uses compound and/or complex sentences.
- Develops more structured paragraphs that include an introduction, a body, and a conclusion.
- Self-edits for complete sentences, use of capitalization, and ending punctuation.
- Correctly spells many basic words.
- Includes more advanced story-writing elements, including use of persuasion, conflict resolution, and dialogue.

The pretty princess said, "Please don't hurt me, Mr. Dragon." The big dragon said, "I would never hurt you, princess. I want to be your friend."

Teaching Beginning Writers

Although young children have a natural tendency to communicate, and may pick up aspects of writing through the reading process, they still need to be taught how to structure their ideas and expand their thinking into related sentences and stories. Ideally, children should be given the opportunity to learn and practice writing skills on a daily basis. Lessons should incorporate a variety of learning styles to best meet the needs of individual students. Teachers should be aware that beginning writers not only progress through five different stages of writing, but through four different performance levels within each stage.

- **Oral Level:** Students demonstrate their understanding of concepts through discussion, dictation, and verbal examples. However, they are not yet ready to express their ideas in writing.

- **Representational Level:** Initially students use drawings and diagrams to organize and describe their thoughts and ideas. As new elements and skills are introduced through teacher modeling and group collaboration, students are able to see how concepts work. They learn how to apply skills by interacting with the teacher as he or she demonstrates and guides the writing process.

- **Independent Level:** Students independently (or with partners) practice and apply a skill learned during direct instruction. They write words, sentences, and eventually stories to accompany their illustrations. Their writing demonstrates a basic understanding of the activity's concepts, and they are learning to apply these concepts and integrate them with previously learned skills.

- **Advanced Level:** Students independently (or with partners) practice and expand on writing concepts. They demonstrate more mature thought processing, and their ideas show a greater degree of sophistication. They not only draw pictures and write words to express their thoughts, they use a combination of skills to elaborate on the concepts taught during direct instruction.

Teaching Tips

The activities presented in this resource book are multilevel—they include instructional guidelines, alternative teaching approaches, and extension activities to help you best meet the needs of a multiability classroom. When teaching the activities, have all students participate in both the oral and representational phases of each lesson. Guide students through the composing process and reinforce proper use of sentence structure and mechanics. This will ensure that all students understand the basic writing concepts presented and will encourage students to share ideas. After direct instruction, continue to help less capable writers as they complete the activity. Use the follow-up suggestions to adapt guided practice and independent work to best meet the needs of upper-level students. In addition, post around the classroom enlarged, colored, and laminated writing charts (see Reproducibles and Resources, pages 69–112) for easy reference and visual guidance. Also consider the following suggestions as you teach writing to your students.

 Stage 1: Focus on the "overall picture" of written communication and story development. Discuss story content, purpose, and structure. Have students identify and describe story components such as characters, setting, plot, and story sequence. Remember that even at this early stage, children benefit from discussing story development, even if they are unable to put their thoughts into writing.

 Stage 2: Focus on having students express and organize thoughts through the use of words and sentences. Identify and discuss sentence components, including word functions (e.g., "naming" words and "doing" words) and the arrangement of words within sentences. Have students manipulate parts of a sentence and practice sentence formation.

 Stage 3: Focus on having students expand ideas to form more complete sentences. Emphasize word functions and how they are used to enhance sentences. Have students form three-part sentences and stories that describe "who," "what," and "where."

 Stage 4: Focus on story development and sequence of events. Emphasize combining and "stretching" sentences to write more complete, detailed stories. Help students work on story transition from one event to the next. Have students compose five-part sentences and stories that describe "who," "what," "where," "when," and "why."

 Stage 5: Focus on having students explore various writing styles and use more sophisticated story elements, such as dialogue, cause-and-effect, and persuasive arguments. Help students develop a distinct "writing voice" and a sense of "audience." Encourage them to self-edit their work, correcting for punctuation, structure, and content.

Writing and Spelling

When students are learning to express themselves, the emphasis should be more on ideas than on mechanics. Children who are permitted and encouraged to "spell it so you can read it" typically write longer, more creative sentences and stories than children who only write words they know how to spell. However, caution must be taken; when "invented spelling" is used over long periods of time, misspellings become a learned pattern. To avoid this problem, spelling lessons should accompany writing instruction. Like writing, spelling is a sequential process that includes different developmental stages: precommunicative spelling, semiphonetic spelling, phonetic spelling, transitional spelling, and, finally, conventional spelling.

Precommunicative and Semiphonetic Spellers

Children attempt to write words long before they understand the principles of spelling. Precommunicative spellers use random scribbles and symbols to communicate their thoughts on paper. They have not yet developed the conceptual understanding that letters of the alphabet represent spoken sounds. As these students mature and are allowed the opportunity to "play with sounds," they enter the next stage of development: semiphonetic spelling. At this phase, children realize that letters represent spoken sounds, which can be blended to form words. However, they have difficulty hearing and recognizing individual sounds within words. Thus, their word spellings are often incomplete. For example, semiphonetic spellers may write the word *where* as *wr*.

Precommunicative and semiphonetic spellers need plenty of exposure to and practice with phonemic-awareness activities in order to progress into the more advanced stages of spelling. They need to be trained to listen for the individual sounds that make up words. When teaching precommunicative and semiphonetic spellers, focus on writing activities that help students segment or split apart words into separate sound units.

Sample Activity: Picture Trains

Use "picture trains" to emphasize how to segment sounds. In the first part of the train (the engine), draw or glue on a picture of an object whose name includes a short vowel sound (consonant-vowel-consonant patterns work best). Then attach a blank boxcar for each sound in the word. Have children look at the picture and count the number of boxcars to identify how many sounds are in the word. Then have them write the corresponding letters that make up the sounds.

Phonetic Spellers

Phonetic spellers sound out words in order to spell them. They do not rely on visual cues. Because various letter combinations represent the same sound, phonetic spellers are frequently inaccurate. For example, they may spell *where* as *whar*. To help these students become better spellers, teach activities that help them compare the way words sound to how they look in print.

Sample Activity: Picture Pockets

Cut out unlabeled picture cards of objects whose names include a short vowel sound. Use a permanent marker to write the name of each object at the bottom of its picture. Fold up and staple the bottom of a laminated index card to form a pocket. Stack the picture cards inside the pocket so that the names are covered. Invite students to use erasable crayons or dry-erase markers to write on the pocket front the name of the picture that is on top of the stack. Have them lift the card out of the pocket to self-check their spelling.

Transitional Spellers

In addition to "sounding out words," transitional spellers rely on visual cues to remember how words look. These students are developing a "memory bank" of high-frequency words for quick and easy recall. The spelling errors these students make typically involve the incorrect use of letter patterns. For example, transitional spellers may write *whair* for the word *where*. To help these students become more accurate spellers, allow plenty of opportunities for them to identify, memorize, and practice writing "sight words"—words used often in writing, or words that follow irregular spelling patterns.

Sample Activity: "Have To" Word Bank

Make a chart of "have to" words (i.e., high-frequency words) for students to refer to as they read and write. List the words in numbered rows of ten. You may choose to add corresponding rebus symbols so emergent writers can easily identify the words. When students ask how to spell these words, send them to the chart to check the spelling themselves. If a child needs more guidance in finding a word on the chart, identify which numbered row the word is in.

(Note: This chart doesn't have to list words in ABC order because teachers may not present them that way. He/she may just tag on the words to the chart as they are learned.)

Conventional Spellers

Conventional spelling is synonymous with accurate spelling. Children at this developmental stage successfully use both auditory and visual cues to remember how to spell words. They are expanding their knowledge and understanding of letter patterns and "word families" to become better spellers. To help these students consistently spell words accurately, teach activities that focus on word parts (e.g., prefixes, suffixes, and parts of compound words), and help students learn different spellings for same sounds (e.g., *ate* and *eight*). Encourage the use of new vocabulary, and help students compare the spelling patterns of new words to those already learned. Finally, stress purposeful writing, as it is one of the most important keys to learning how to spell.

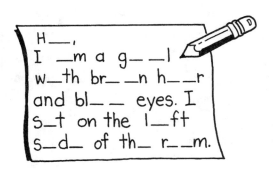

Sample Activity: Secret Messages

Write and photocopy simple sentences or a short story about a theme-related topic or classroom event. Then delete word parts, and draw a writing line for each omitted letter. Invite students to fill in the blanks to discover the "secret message."

Handling Handwriting

To avoid putting young children on "overload" by expecting good handwriting in addition to thoughtful, sequential stories, initiate handwriting instruction before teaching writing. By the time students are ready to begin writing sentences and stories, their handwriting skills will already be established.

At the beginning of the school year, have students concentrate on letter size, letter formation, directionality, and spacing. Use a comical stick figure ("Charlie the Line Man") to introduce the three boundary lines used to guide letter formation—the head line (touching the top of Charlie's head), the middle line (corresponding to Charlie's belt), and the foot line (the line Charlie is standing on).

Teach "rounded letters" first (e.g., *a, c, e, o,* and *s*), followed by "uh oh" backtrack letters (e.g., *b, d, g, h, m, n, p, q,* and *r*), "stick letters" (e.g., *f, i, k, l,* and *t*), "tail letters" (e.g., *j* and *y*), and finally "zig-zag" letters (e.g., *v, w, x,* and *z*). When introducing the first "uh oh" letter, share the following story to encourage the use of continuous strokes and to reduce letter-reversal problems:

"Uh-Oh" Story

One day your mom takes you on a drive to the ice-cream store. On the way there, she misses the street and says, "Uh oh! I missed my turn." Does she get out of the car, pick it up, and go back to the turn? No, she just backs up. So, when you're writing the "uh oh" letters that have a turn, don't stop and pick up your "car" (pencil); just back up with your pencil and make the turn.

Teach only one or two letters at a time, and allow plenty of opportunities for whole-group and independent practice. During direct instruction, have students draw a green dot to designate the starting point of a letter; this will help prevent oversized print and letter reversals. Have them write rows of the same letter and then circle the one they think looks best. Once students have had adequate practice making individual letters, help them write words and then sentences. For students having difficulty spacing out words, draw boxes on the lines for them to write the words in.

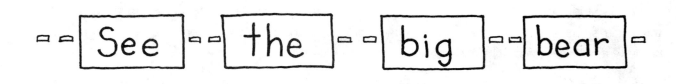

Helping ESL Students

ESL students will benefit from the oral component of the activities in this resource book. They will learn how to verbally expand sentences and stories by describing "who," "what," "where," "when," and "why." Because the activities emphasize sentence formation, students who are learning the English language will develop a better understanding of syntax, word order, and what is needed to make a complete sentence. They will also learn word functions as well as proper use of "connector words" (i.e., prepositions, articles, and conjunctions). One of the best benefits for ESL learners is being able to participate in the same activities as the rest of the class, which will help the students receive support and encouragement from their peers.

Record-Keeping and Assessment

Use the Performance Checkoff sheets (pages 69 and 70) to assess and evaluate students' progress as they advance through the different levels and stages of writing. Use these assessment charts during student-teacher or parent-teacher conferences to discuss the student's accomplishments and current writing needs. In addition to the assessments that you've written, have students use simplified checklist sheets to self-assess and partner-edit stories. Include questions such as *Does the story make sense? Is there a main character? Do the sentences have capital letters? Do the sentences have end marks?* For extra fun, staple stacks of checklist sheets to cardboard backings to make "checklist necklaces" for students to wear as they circulate and share their stories with partners. (See the illustration below.) Have pairs listen to and look at each other's stories. Then ask each "listening partner" to use the top sheet of his or her necklace to check off information about his or her partner's story. Instruct the "reading partner" to take the completed sheet and store it inside a pocket stapled to the back of his or her checklist necklace. Review the completed sheet with the student during an individual conference.

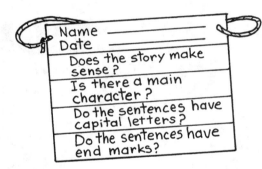

Parent Involvement

Parents play an important role in the development of writing skills in young children. Family discussions, storytelling, and shared reading experiences are ideal segues to language exploration and story development. Encourage parent involvement by sending home letters (see pages 16–18) that describe the writing process and offer activities for children and their parents to complete together.

Dear Parents,

Attached is a list of "have to" words that your child is learning in class. These high-frequency words are ones children tend to use over and over again as they write. There is no easy way for children to remember these "sight words"; the best way is by repetitively seeing them in print. You can help your child learn these words by spending time together reading and writing. Here are just a few ways to turn learning time into fun time:

- Write eight to ten "have to" words on an erasable memo board that is hung on your refrigerator. Every time your child sees or hears one of the sight words during shared reading or storytelling, ask him or her to spell the word aloud. If the word is spelled correctly, erase it from the list. Reward your child when all the words have been erased from the board. Repeat the process with other "have to" words.

- Write on paper (or on an erasable memo board) some simple, silly sentences. Erase all the high-frequency words. Invite your child to select words from the "have to" list to fill in the blanks. Compare and discuss the "sense" and "nonsense" sentences that your child formed.

- Use the "Have To" Words sheet to play "Four in a Row" with your child. Copy each word onto a separate index card, and then place the stack of cards facedown on a table. Take turns selecting cards from the pile and matching them to words on the sheet. Have one player mark the words he or she selects by drawing a circle around the matching word on the list; have the other player draw a square to mark his or her words. The first person to mark four words that are in a row wins the game.

- Use "have to" words to play a game of "Concentration." Make two matching sets of high-frequency word cards. Place the cards facedown on a table. Take turns flipping over pairs of cards to find matches. When a player uncovers a match, he or she must say a sentence that includes the word.

"Have To" Words

about	going	made	then
after	good	make	there
and	had	my	they
are	has	name	this
as	have	next	we
at	he	not	went
before	her	of	what
but	here	on	when
can	him	play	where
come	in	said	who
could	is	see	why
do	it	she	will
for	know	that	with
from	like	the	would
go	look	them	you

Teaching Beginning Writing © 1999 Creative Teaching Press

Dear Parents,

Your child is learning to write descriptive sentences that describe "who," "what," "where," "when," and "why." Soon he or she will be learning how to expand sentences into vivid and intriguing stories that have a beginning, a middle, and an end. You can help your child's writing progress by discussing key parts of a story, identifying new vocabulary words, and helping him or her discover meaningful topics to write about. The following activities are just a few ways to help your child develop a love of writing:

- Have your child observe and read printed materials in your environment, such as food labels, road signs, newspaper advertisements, and amusement-park signs. Look for ways in which your child can write about people and objects in and around your home. For example, have your child write a new commercial about a favorite food, replace the dialogue in a comic strip, write invitations to a family function, or use cutout words from junk-mail advertisements to form sentences.

- Read aloud and discuss stories to help your child understand general story structure. Ask your child questions about key elements of the story—who the character is, what he or she looks like, where and when the story takes place, what events happened, and why the events happened. Encourage your child to visualize the images being described and to identify specific words and sentences that help the story "come alive." Invite your child to retell the story and summarize the beginning, middle, and end.

- Work together to complete a "topics chart" that your child can use to preplan stories to be written at home or in class. Include the following categories: *Friends, Family, Favorite Activities, Special Places, Special Holidays, Special Traditions, Hobbies or Sports,* and *Pets.* Help your child think of topics to list underneath the different headers. On a regular basis, invite your child to select a topic from the list to write about. Make a copy of the topics chart for your child to bring to school so that he or she has several ideas to choose from when asked to write a story.

- Invite your child to secretly write descriptive sentences about favorite people, places, or things. Then have him or her read the sentences aloud as you draw a picture to match the words. Show the picture to your child, and ask if the drawing is what he or she had in mind. Help your child revise the sentences to be more descriptive and to better match his or her thoughts. Switch roles and repeat the process.

Teaching Beginning Writing © 1999 Creative Teaching Press

Story Log

Make photocopies and a transparency of the Story Log sheet. Introduce a story by describing the main characters and the setting. Invite students to close their eyes and visualize what is being described. Place the Story Log transparency on an overhead projector, and draw in the appropriate boxes simple pictures of the characters and the setting. Explain that the three remaining boxes will be filled in after the story is read. Ask students to listen carefully as you read the story aloud, having them pay close attention to the sequence of events—what happens at the beginning, in the middle, and at the end of the story. As you read the story aloud, stop and discuss key events to help students keep track of the story sequence. After reading the story, give each student a copy of the Story Log sheet. Have students refer to your illustrations as they draw pictures of the characters and the setting. Use the transparency to guide students as they draw pictures of what happened at the beginning (box 1), in the middle (box 2), and at the end (box 3) of the story. (Note: Tell students to draw simple illustrations— e.g., stick figures and simple shapes—so that the focus of the lesson is on the story content.) Invite volunteers to retell the story using their pictures as a reference.

Materials

- primary story that has a clear beginning, middle, and end
- Story Log sheet (page 71)
- overhead projector, transparency, and markers
- crayons or markers

Objectives

- Listen for and identify key events in a story read aloud.
- Identify which story events occur at the beginning, in the middle, and at the end.
- Identify the story setting and key characters.
- Draw pictures to represent the key events in a story.

Extension: Repeat the process with other stories. Depending on their ability level, have students discuss the stories and complete story logs collaboratively, dictate sentences to go along with their pictures, or independently write their own corresponding words and sentences.

Do It Yourself

In advance, draw pictures of a character and a setting on a Story Log sheet. Make photocopies of the sheet, and distribute them to individual students, partners, or small groups. Ask each student (or team of students) to make up a story that includes the given character and setting. Remind students that their stories must include three parts—a beginning, a middle, and an end. Have them draw pictures on the log sheet of what happens first, next, and last. Invite students to share their stories. Compare and contrast the variations in story theme and sequence.

Materials

- Story Log sheet (page 71)
- crayons or markers

Objectives

- Make up a story about a specific character in a particular setting.
- Structure a story so that it has a beginning, a middle, and an end.
- Work with others to develop and illustrate a story.

Variation: Use an overhead transparency to develop a collaborative story with students. Invite each student to draw his or her own illustrations for the group story.

Extension: In addition to providing the character and the setting, describe how the story begins (or invite a volunteer to decide the first event). Then ask students to determine how the rest of the story evolves. This approach will help demonstrate the divergence of story development.

Backward Stories

In advance, copy each sentence from the Story Endings sheet onto a separate index card. For extra motivation and learning for all, have an upper-grade class write additional story endings for this activity. Place the index cards in a grab bag. Give each student a photocopy of the Story Log sheet. Select a card from the bag, and read aloud the story ending. Model how to build a story "backwards," brainstorming events that could have led to the selected ending. Ask partners to select a card and develop their own story to fit the ending. Have students draw "beginning," "middle," and "end" pictures on their log sheet. Invite students to share their stories with the upper-grade students who wrote the endings.

Materials

- Story Endings sheet (page 72)
- index cards
- grab bag
- Story Log sheet (page 71)
- crayons or markers

Objectives

- Complete the beginning and middle portions of a story given its ending.
- Identify cause-and-effect relationships in a story.
- Share stories orally and through illustrations.

Variation: Have the class reconstruct a familiar story or create a story collaboratively before working independently. Each student can then complete his or her own log sheet of the group's story. For extra reinforcement and fun, invite students to tape-record their stories.

Extension: On chart paper, write out a story as the class develops it together. Use the written story for a choral reading activity.

Line 'Em Up

In advance, write the beginning, middle, and end of a short story on separate pieces of chart paper. Select one or two students to hold up each page in random order. Explain to the class that you have a three-page story, but you can't remember the order to put the pages in. Ask students to think of a solution. Offer prompts until students reach the conclusion that reading the pages is the best approach. Have the class read each page aloud to determine the correct story sequence. Line up the students holding the pages so that the story appears in sequential order. Then have the class reread the story in proper sequence.

Materials

- short story with a clear beginning, middle, and end
- chart paper
- marker

Objectives

- Identify the beginning, middle, and end of a story.
- Unscramble written story text so that it is in proper sequence.
- Match parts of a story read aloud to corresponding written text.

Extension: Provide laminated story pages that students can independently sequence. Include pictures with some of the text to accommodate lower-level learners. Number the pages on the back so that the students can self-check their work. To avoid mix-ups, use different colored numbers (or construction-paper backing) for each story.

Cut and Tell

In advance, have the class help you create story logs of several favorite primary stories. Cover the numbers in the picture boxes. You may also choose to have older students or parent volunteers help complete the sheets. (As a time-saver, make photocopies of the completed story logs and save the extra sets for use in later activities.) Color-code and laminate the sheets. Cut apart the pictures for each story, and place them in a matching color-coded envelope. Distribute the envelopes to individual students, partners, or small groups. Ask students to look at their pictures, put them in sequential order, and decide which story corresponds to the illustrations. Invite volunteers to use the picture prompts to help retell the story aloud. (Note: Initially, students may recount the stories with minimal detail. However, with prompting and guided practice, they will learn to elaborate on story events.)

Materials

- favorite primary stories
- Story Log sheet (page 71)
- markers
- scissors
- envelopes

Objectives

- Arrange pictures in proper story sequence.
- Retell a story.

Variation: For more advanced learners, provide corresponding topic sentences along with the pictures. Have them match the sentences with the illustrations as they place the parts in proper sequence. Ask students to elaborate on what has been written so that the story is more complete.

Extension: To demonstrate how to put thoughts down on paper, write on chart paper the stories students retell aloud, or select one of the stories for students to retell and write down collaboratively.

In the Beginning

In advance, copy each In the Beginning "story starter" onto a separate large index card. (You may choose to have older students or parent volunteers write additional story starters.) Introduce the activity by reading one of the story starters aloud. Explain to the class that they are to "fill in the blanks" to complete the story. Reread the first sentence, and identify it as the *topic sentence*—a sentence that identifies *who* or *what* the story is about. Reread the next part of the text, and explain that these "linking words" indicate that something in the story is about to change. Reread the last word of the story starter, and explain that its role is to tell the reader that the story is about to end. Invite students to suggest sentences that you can use to fill in the blanks of the story. Emphasize that every story has a beginning, a middle, and an end. Repeat the process with additional story-starter cards. For extra fun, invite students to draw pictures to go along with the stories they create.

Materials

- In the Beginning sheets (pages 73–74)
- large index cards
- crayons or markers (optional)

Objectives

- Use story starters to build a plot that has a beginning, a middle, and an end.
- Identify topic sentences and "linking words" that indicate transition from one part of a story to the next.
- Combine and elaborate on given details to present a more complete story.

Variation: Write additional story starters that include other linking words and phrases, such as *later, the next day, at the end,* and *finally.*

Extension: After a story has been developed orally, invite students to help write it on the chalkboard or on chart paper. Encourage them to sound out the words and add the necessary punctuation. Invite more advanced learners to find transitional words in favorite storybooks.

Mix and Match

In advance, fill out and laminate several story logs of favorite primary stories (or use extra story logs made in previous activities). Cut apart the numbered pictures, but leave the character and setting boxes attached together as a strip. Place sets of four stories into separate envelopes. Divide the class into groups of four, and give each team a packet of stories. Ask group members to each select a character/setting strip and then place the other cards facedown in a pile. Have students take turns introducing their character and identifying the setting of their story. After sharing this information, ask group members to take turns selecting cards from the pile, one card at a time. The group decides together who has the corresponding character/setting strip, and then gives the selected card to that student. The process continues—arranging the cards in proper sequence—until all four picture stories are complete. Conclude the activity by inviting groups to tell the rest of the class about the stories they've pieced together.

Materials
- Story Log sheet (page 71)
- crayons or markers
- scissors
- large envelopes

Objectives
- Use picture prompts to identify and describe story sequence.
- Group together pictures that refer to the same topic.
- Assemble the parts of a story in proper sequence.
- Identify mismatched and unrelated story parts.

Variation: Instead of cutting up the story logs, make corresponding sentence cards. Distribute the story logs, and have group members take turns selecting sentence cards and matching them to the correct pictures. The winner is the first student to match all three sentences to his or her pictures.

Story Detectives

In advance, make a transparency of the Story Detectives sheet, and display it on an overhead projector. Have each student write *B, M,* and *E* on separate index cards. Explain to students that stories contain "clue words" that help identify the order in which events occur. Give examples of common transitional words and phrases, such as *first, finally, meanwhile, the next day,* and *as a result.* Then have the class read aloud the first sentence on the transparency. Ask students to hold up the card that indicates whether the sentence belongs at the beginning *(B),* middle *(M),* or end *(E)* of a story. Have them identify which word or words helped them make their decision. Invite a volunteer to write *B, M,* or *E* in front of the sentence on the transparency. Repeat the process with the other sentences.

Materials

- Story Detectives sheet (page 75)
- overhead projector, transparency, and marker
- index cards

Objectives

- Identify "clue words" (transitional words) that indicate progression through time and help introduce, develop, and conclude a story.

- Determine whether a specific event occurs in the beginning, middle, or end of a story.

Extension: Invite more advanced writers to plan, organize, and write a story based on a selected story clue.

Highlighter's Delight

In advance, use a black permanent marker to write a short story on chart paper or on an overhead transparency. (Copy a favorite big book, or have students help you write about a special classroom event, such as a field trip or a school assembly.) Display the story, and use a left-to-right hand sweep under the sentences to guide students as they read the story aloud. Number the sentences, and point out the proper punctuation and capitalization used in each one. Ask students questions about what happened at the beginning, middle, and end of the story. Invite volunteers to highlight the "beginning" sentences in green, the "middle" sentences in blue, and the "end" sentences in pink. (Refer to the numbers in front of the sentences when guiding students' responses.) After all the sentences have been highlighted, reread the story to emphasize how the different parts fit together to form a story.

Materials

- short story
- chart paper or an overhead projector and transparency
- black permanent marker
- green, blue, and pink highlighters

Objectives

- Identify whether specific sentences belong in the beginning, middle, or end of a story.
- Use proper capitalization and end punctuation.

Variation: In addition to the chart-paper copy or transparency, write the story on regular paper, and make a photocopy for each student. As the sentences on the chart paper are being highlighted, ask students to use green, blue, and red crayons or markers to underline the corresponding text on their paper.

Extension: Provide additional stories for students to highlight independently. Introduce more advanced learners to the concept of paragraph formation. Have them identify which paragraphs comprise the beginning, the middle, and the end of the story.

Secretary Pool

In advance, recruit parent volunteers or an upper-grade class to help with this activity. Brief the helpers on their responsibilities as a "secretary": to write down on paper the sentences a student dictates aloud, to ask their "boss" (the student) for help in spelling out words and punctuating sentences, and to read back the written sentences for their boss's approval. Pair up students with volunteers. Give each student his or her completed story log from a previous lesson. Then tell students to play "boss" and retell their stories as their secretaries write down what they say. Encourage secretaries to prompt and question their bosses, asking them what comes first, next, and last in the story; requesting help sounding out and spelling words; and confirming proper use of capitalization and end punctuation. (You may wish to write these prompts on the chalkboard for helpers to refer to.) Circulate around the room and monitor progress as students dictate their stories. After the secretaries "clock out" (finish their responsibilities), invite students to read aloud their written stories.

Materials

- completed Story Logs from a recent lesson
- writing paper

Objectives

- Refer to picture prompts to help retell a story.
- Write sentences that correspond to picture prompts.
- Strengthen print awareness by identifying letter/sound correspondence, practicing left-to-right sequencing, and using basic punctuation (i.e., capitalization and end marks).

Variation: Invite more advanced learners to pair up and take turns playing the role of boss and secretary. Offer secretaries the option of using "shorthand" (drawing pictures) instead of writing words.

Build a Sentence

Enlarge, color, and laminate the Build a Sentence chart, and post it on a chalkboard or a bulletin board. To visually remind students about sentence punctuation, color the capital *S* green and the period red. Use this "picture reminder" to help teach students the parts of a sentence. As you say the subject or the "naming" words, point to the first illustration; as you say the verb or the "doing" words, point to the second. Once students understand the relationship between a two-part sentence and the graphics, invite them to complete partial sentences you say aloud. First provide the subject and have students supply the action. Use students' names to personalize the sentences. After several examples, reverse the process and provide the predicate. Continue pointing to the appropriate visuals as students respond to the prompts.

Materials

- Build a Sentence chart (page 76)
- crayons or markers

Objectives

- Identify the subject ("naming" words) and predicate ("doing" words) of a sentence.
- Write a two-part sentence that contains a noun and a verb.
- Self-check and correct the structure of a sentence.

A dog   eats food

Extension: Invite students to cut out action pictures from magazines and newspapers. Then use a simple sentence to describe each cutout (or invite more advanced learners to describe their own pictures). Ask the class to identify the "naming" and "doing" parts of each sentence.

Half Sentences

In advance, use tape or flat magnets to attach the colored, laminated Build a Sentence chart onto a chalkboard. Alongside the chart, write on the chalkboard the incomplete sentences listed on the Half Sentences sheet. (Be sure to leave enough space for the missing words.) Refer to the graphics on the Build a Sentence chart as you review with students the parts of a sentence. Explain that the sentences listed on the chalkboard are only partially complete—that either the subject ("somebody or something") or the predicate ("doing or being") is missing. Invite students to play a "whodunit" game by having them use their imagination to decide which subject or predicate is missing from each sentence. Invite students to share their answers aloud as you write the corresponding words on the chalkboard. Complete the activity by having volunteers draw separate boxes around the subject and the predicate of each sentence.

Materials

- tape or flat magnets
- Build a Sentence chart (see activity, page 29)
- Half Sentences sheet (page 77)
- chalkboard and chalk

Objectives

- Identify the subject and the predicate of a simple sentence.
- Complete a two-part sentence that describes "who is doing what."

Variation: Invite students to use chalk to complete the sentences written on the chalkboard. Accept invented spelling, as the lesson is about sentence formation. Have more advanced learners complete a photocopy of the Half Sentences sheet.

Extension: Divide the class into partners, and have each pair write their own "whodunit" sentence. Ask one student in each pair to write the "who" portion of the sentence and his or her partner to write the "doing what." Invite students to share their sentences with the rest of the class. (Note: When pairing students, match lower-level writers with more advanced ones to encourage peer-tutoring.)

Pop-Up Sentences

In advance, use "Who" and "Doing What" Picture Cards and manila folders to make Pop-Up Sentence folders. Cut two side-by-side rectangular windows in the front of a folder, and label the two flaps *Who* and *Doing What.* Tape a corresponding "who" and "doing what" picture card behind each window so that the picture is displayed when the flap is lifted. Open the folder and staple a construction-paper pocket inside to hold completed sentence strips that the children will be writing. To begin the lesson, attach a Pop-Up Sentence folder to the chalkboard, and have the class sit close by. Explain to students that every sentence must include a subject ("who") and an action phrase ("doing what"). Invite a volunteer to lift up the flaps to display the pictures, and have the class read aloud the corresponding words. Ask students if reading the two words together sounds like a complete sentence. Invite another volunteer to make a sentence using the two words. Write the sentence on the chalkboard, and identify the "connector words" (e.g., articles, prepositions, adjectives, direct objects) needed to complete the sentence and make it "sound right." Repeat the process with other Pop-Up Sentence folders, inviting volunteers to write the suggested sentences on the chalkboard.

Materials

- "Who" and "Doing What" Picture Cards (pages 78–85)
- supplies for Pop-Up Sentence folders (manila folders, scissors, markers, tape, construction paper, stapler)
- chalkboard and chalk

Objectives

- Construct two-part sentences that describe "someone doing something."
- Use encoding skills and "connector words" to form complete sentences.

Extension: Have individual students or partners use Pop-Up Sentence folders during independent practice. Have them write their sentences on 8" (20 cm) sentence-strip pieces and then place the completed sentences inside the paper pocket for other students to read and enjoy.

Pull-Through Sentences

This activity works best when taught in small groups. In advance, cut 12" (30.5 cm) and 8" (20 cm) sentence-strip pieces. On each 12" strip, write an incomplete sentence that is missing either the simple subject or the verb; for example, *The _____ rides in a car.* Then cut two slits in the 12" strip so that an 8" strip can be pulled or woven through, as shown in the illustration. Select one of the 12" strips (with the 8" strip removed), and read aloud the incomplete sentence. Invite the group to brainstorm "naming" words or "doing" words (whichever is appropriate) to fill in the blank. Discuss which words would make sense in the sentence and which would not. For example, *The <u>horse</u> rides in a car* is not realistic. Use students' suggestions to write a column of words down the 8" strip. (Note: The height of each word should match the height of the words used in the sentence.) Demonstrate how to insert the 8" strip and pull it through the 12" strip to form complete sentences. Invite students to read aloud each new sentence as it is formed. Repeat the process with other pull-through sentence patterns.

Materials
- sentence strips
- scissors
- marker

Objectives
- Form pattern sentences, each of which contains a subject and an action phrase.
- Identify sense and nonsense sentences.

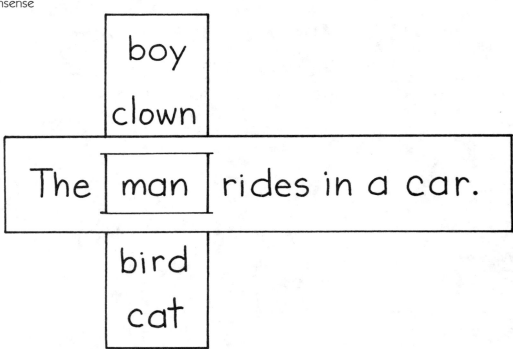

Variation: Provide precut pieces for students to make their own pull-through sentences. To reuse the patterns, laminate the pieces and have students write with erasable crayons or dry-erase markers.

Creating Captions

In advance, collect assorted action pictures, each of which shows a character completing an activity. Number the pictures and post them around the classroom. Distribute writing paper and a clipboard or an individual chalkboard to each student. Review with the class how to write a sentence, including the important role of "connector" words. Define and give examples of a caption—a sentence that describes "somebody doing something." Invite students to walk around the classroom and look at the pictures. Then ask them to write captions on their paper for some or all of the posted pictures. (The amount they write depends on their ability level.) Remind students to start each sentence with a capital letter and end it with a period. Have them number their captions to correspond to the numbers written on the pictures. At the end of the activity, point to each picture, and invite students to share the corresponding captions they've written.

Materials

- assorted action pictures (e.g., theme-related pictures and simple cartoons)
- writing paper and clipboards or individual chalkboards

Objectives

- Write two-part sentences to describe pictures.
- Select "connector" words to join together parts of a sentence.

Variation: Write on the chalkboard a list of words for students to select from when writing their captions. For extra guidance, identify the words as "naming" words, "doing" words, and "connector" words. Encourage more advanced learners to write lengthier sentences that include descriptive words, such as those that describe the size, shape, and color of the objects and people in the pictures.

Color-Coded Sentences

In advance, write a list of simple sentences, each of which contains a subject and a verb. Make photocopies of the sentences for students. Write the words *Who* and *Doing What* on separate large index cards or reusable stick-on notes, and post the labels high up on the chalkboard. Invite a volunteer to pantomime an action; for example, reading a book. Ask the class to identify what the student is doing. Then have the volunteer stand underneath the *Who* label as you draw below the *Doing What* label a picture of the action displayed. Remind the class that a sentence describes "somebody doing something." Write on the chalkboard a sentence that describes what the volunteer dramatized (e.g., *Josh is reading a book*). Ask students to read the sentence aloud as you use different colored chalk to circle the subject and underline the predicate. Repeat the process a few more times with new volunteers. Then give each student two crayons or colored pencils and a photocopy of the sentences (made prior to teaching the activity). Tell students to use one colored crayon or pencil to circle the "who" in each sentence, and the other crayon or pencil to underline the "doing what." (Depending on students' writing abilities, complete the activity orally, complete it as a whole group, or have students work independently.)

Materials

- writing paper
- large index cards or reusable stick-on notes
- chalkboard and colored chalk
- crayons or colored pencils

Objectives

- Read and write two-part sentences.
- Identify the subject and the predicate in a sentence.

Extension: More advanced writers can expand the sentences by adding describing words to each one.

Match 'Em Up

In advance, write on the chalkboard two adjacent lists of nouns and verbs. Have the class read the words aloud. Invite students to help you pair up words from each column to form sentences. First, ask a volunteer to select a word from the "who" (noun) list. Next, have a second volunteer select a word from the "doing what" (verb) list. Draw a line connecting the two words on the chalkboard, and ask the class to read the two words together. Then invite students to share aloud sentences that include the selected words. Have them identify the "connector words" needed to complete each sentence. In addition, point out sentences that make sense versus those that do not. Continue the activity until all the nouns and the verbs have been paired up.

Materials

- list of nouns and verbs
- chalkboard and chalk

Objectives

- Combine a subject and a predicate to form a complete sentence.
- Identify sense and nonsense sentences.

Variation: Invite students to brainstorm nouns and verbs to be used for the activity.

Extension: Invite more advanced learners to write their own sentences. For extra learning, include the listed "who" and "doing what" words as part of the class spelling list.

35

Scrambled Sentences

Photocopy, laminate, and cut apart the "Who" and "Doing What" Picture Cards. Pair each "who" picture card with a "doing what" picture card, and compose a corresponding sentence for each pair. For example, write *A monkey climbs a tree* for the pictures representing "monkey" and "climbs." Write each needed "connector word" on a separate index card. Group together the picture and word cards for each sentence, and use an erasable crayon to number the back of each card according to sentence sequence (for easier management and clean-up, use a different colored crayon for each set of cards). Store the cards needed for each sentence in a separate envelope, and color-code the envelopes to match the colored numbers. To start the lesson, place one set of cards in random order on the top line of a pocket chart. Show students how to use the picture clues to unscramble the cards and form a sentence that describes "who is doing what." Place a second set of scrambled cards on the next line of the pocket chart. Invite volunteers to help you arrange the cards in proper sequence. Then have the class read the unscrambled sentence aloud and identify the subject and the action words. Continue with additional sentence packs. For extra fun, invite students to create new sentences by interchanging the nouns and verbs of different sentences.

Materials

- "Who" and "Doing What" Picture Cards (pages 78–85)
- scissors
- index cards
- marker
- erasable crayons
- large envelopes
- pocket chart

Objectives

- Use subject and verb picture cards to form phrases.
- Expand phrases to form complete sentences.

Variation: Have students write on paper the sentences formed in the pocket chart. For extra learning, cover up the words written on the picture cards so students have to segment the letter sounds to spell the words.

Extension: Regroup and renumber the picture and word cards to form new sentence packs. Or use magazine cutouts and students' illustrations to make additional sets. Invite students to sequence the cards independently, using the numbers on the back of the cards to check their work.

Flip-Open Fun

In advance, photocopy a supply of Flip-Open Fun sheets. Draw "who" and "doing what" pictures inside one of the copies to use as an example for guided instruction. Fold the sample sheet in half (so that only the pictures show), and hang the paper on an easel or chalkboard for easy viewing. Ask students to identify the pictures and then think of corresponding sentences (i.e., "someone doing something"). Write one of the suggested sentences on the line at the bottom of the page. Remove the sample sheet from the easel, and show students how to fold the paper to make "who" and "doing what" flip-open flaps. Distribute a copy of the Flip-Open Fun sheet to each student or pair to complete. Guide students as they write two-part sentences to describe their illustrations. Invite students to exchange and share their completed Flip-Open Fun sentences.

Materials

- Flip-Open Fun sheet (page 90)
- crayons or markers
- easel or chalkboard

Objectives

- Draw pictures to correspond with two-part sentences that explain "who is doing what."
- Write two-part sentences that describe the pictures.

Variation: Invite students to use reproducible picture cards (pages 78–85) instead of drawings to complete their Flip-Open Fun sheets.

Extension: Invite small groups of students to write different sentences that describe the same Flip-Open Fun sheet. For each student, staple a folded and illustrated Flip-Open Fun sheet to a sheet of writing paper. Have each student write on the first line of the writing paper a sentence that describes the "who" and "doing what" illustrations. Then ask group members to trade Flip-Open Fun sheets and write a new sentence below the one already written. Have students repeat the process until each Flip-Open Fun sheet has a variety of sentences written below it.

Switcheroo

Face the class and use your right hand to display a picture card or magazine cutout of a person or an animal; with your left hand, hold up a picture card or magazine cutout of an action (e.g., a person riding a bicycle). Say a simple sentence that describes the two images combined together; for example, *The boy rides a bicycle.* Remind students that a sentence describes "someone doing something." Then switch the position of the two pictures. Explain to students that some sentences pull a "switcheroo"—they describe the "doing what" before the "who." Give an example of an inverted sentence that describes the two pictures; for example, *After riding his bike, the boy was tired.* Repeat the process with other picture pairs, asking students to help form "switcheroo" sentences that begin with the word *After.* For extra fun, invite volunteers to supply simple sentences for the rest of the class to invert.

Materials

- "Who" and "Doing What" Picture Cards (pages 78–85)
- magazine cutouts of people and objects (optional)

Objectives

- Form sentences by interpreting pictures.
- Rearrange pictures to produce sentences that begin with an action phrase.

After riding his bike, the boy was tired.

Extension: Provide a list of other "switcheroo" words (e.g., *before, while, since,* and *as*) for students to use to form additional inverted sentences. Invite more advanced learners to independently (or with a partner) practice forming "switcheroo" sentences.

Imagination Time

In advance, make photocopies and a transparency of the Imagination Time sheet. Display the transparency on an overhead projector, and write "who," "doing what," and "where" words inside the appropriate circles; for example, *boy, flies a kite,* and *park.* Explain to students that some sentences describe more than just "someone doing something"; they also specify where the action is taking place. Read aloud the words written in the circles, and then have the class brainstorm sentences that include those words. Ask students to identify the "connector words" needed to form the sentences. Prompt students to think of descriptive words that will help you draw a corresponding picture; for example, *Is the kite red or blue? Is the boy big or little?* As you draw the picture, say the corresponding descriptive sentence (e.g., *The little boy flies the red kite at the park*). Distribute a photocopy of the Imagination Time sheet to each student, and suggest additional "who," "doing what," and "where" words for students to write in the circles. Reuse the transparency to guide students as they complete their worksheet. (Have more advanced learners complete the worksheet independently.) Invite students to share their pictures and sentences.

Materials

- Imagination Time sheet (page 91)
- overhead projector, transparency, markers, and wipe cloth
- crayons or markers

Objectives

- Identify nouns that can be described by specific sets of adjectives.
- Write three-part sentences that describe "who is doing what" and "where."

Variation: Invite each student to select "who," "doing what," and "where" word cards (or picture cards; see pages 78–88) from a grab bag. Ask students to draw a picture that corresponds to the words selected.

Extension: Give each student an Imagination Time sheet. Have students complete the top two sections of the sheet (the word circles and the picture) and then exchange papers with a partner. Ask partners to write a sentence to go along with the word and picture "clues" given.

Who Did What Where?

In advance, select some of the picture cards to photocopy, laminate, and cut apart. Write the words *Who, Doing What,* and *Where* on separate index cards, and place the word cards in the top row of a pocket chart. Give each student three index cards on which to write *Who, Doing What,* and *Where.* Show the class the picture cards, one at a time. Ask students to hold up the word card that identifies whether the picture depicts "who," "doing what," or "where." Invite volunteers to place each picture below the appropriate label in the pocket chart. After all the pictures have been sorted, ask a volunteer to select a set of three picture cards—one card from each category. Arrange the cards in proper sequence in the pocket chart, and invite students to brainstorm corresponding three-part sentences. Discuss whether or not the sentences make sense, and ask the class to identify the "connector words" used to complete each one. Repeat the process with other sets of picture cards.

Materials

- "Who," "Doing What," and "Where" Picture Cards (pages 78–88)
- scissors
- index cards
- marker
- pocket chart

Objectives

- Categorize pictures as "who," "doing what," and "where" words.
- Use picture prompts to help form three-part sentences.

Extension: Write "connector words" on separate index cards, and use them with the picture cards to form sentences. Have students read aloud and copy the sentences formed in the pocket chart.

Super Pop-Ups

To make Super Pop-Ups, follow the same procedure used to construct Pop-Up Sentences (see page 31), except include a third flip-up flap and corresponding picture that identifies "where" (see sample sentences on page 89). Explain to students that these Super Pop-Ups not only describe "who is doing what," but they also tell where the action is taking place. Attach one of the pop-up folders to the chalkboard, and flip up the *Who* flap to reveal whom the sentence is about. Then invite students to predict what the character is doing as you list their ideas on the chalkboard. Invite a volunteer to flip up the *Doing What* flap to see if any of the predictions were correct. Repeat the process for the *Where* flap to reveal all three pictures. Then ask individuals or partners to write on paper a sentence that describes the pop-up pictures. Invite students to share their sentences aloud as you write their suggestions on the chalkboard. Discuss and compare the variety of sentences formed. As a group, brainstorm adjectives and adverbs to add to the sentences to make them more descriptive. Repeat the process with other Super Pop-Ups.

Materials

- "Who," "Doing What," and "Where" Picture Cards (pages 78–88)
- Sample Picture-Card Sentences sheet (page 89)
- manila folders
- markers
- tape
- chalkboard and chalk
- writing paper

Objectives

- Construct three-part sentences that describe "who is doing what" and "where."
- Use encoding skills and "connector words" to form complete sentences.

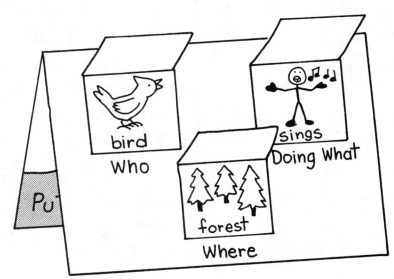

Variation: Use seasonal, theme-related, or nursery-rhyme pictures as visual prompts for Super Pop-Ups. Invite students to make their own pop-up folders by having them draw or glue appropriate pictures behind the flip-up flaps.

Extension: Invite more advanced learners to expand their three-part sentences into three-part stories. Have them write paragraphs that describe "who is doing what" and "where."

Stand-Up Sentences

In advance, write on paper a list of three-part sentences. Use construction paper, a marker, a hole punch, and yarn to make for the class color-coded *Who, Doing What,* and *Where* necklaces (e.g., use blue construction paper for all *Who* necklaces). Divide the class into groups of three, and distribute a set of *Who, Doing What,* and *Where* necklaces to each group to wear. (Invite "left-over" students to be your helpers.) Explain to the class that good writers sometimes make sentences more interesting by switching the order of "who," "doing what," and "where." For example, *The boy eats popcorn at the movies* can be rearranged to form the sentence *At the movies, the boy eats popcorn.* Ask groups to do the following: listen to each sentence you say aloud; decide the order of "who," "doing what," and "where"; and then stand in the order that matches the sequence of the sentence. Read aloud a sentence from the list (you may wish to rearrange the order of the parts before sharing the sentence aloud), and ask one group to demonstrate the process. Then invite the rest of the class to join in the fun. After groups arrange themselves, share (or have a helper share) the correct sequence, and have a volunteer write the corresponding sentence on the chalkboard. Repeat the process with other sentences.

Materials

- writing paper
- construction paper, three different colors
- marker
- hole punch
- yarn
- chalkboard and chalk

Objectives

- Compose three-part sentences.
- Experiment with word sequence in three-part sentences.

Variation: Have groups write the sentence you say aloud before they stand up to show the "who," "doing what," and "where" sequence. Or ask students to copy the sentences from the chalkboard at the end of the activity.

Extension: Invite students to write additional "stand-up" sentences, to be used the next time the class completes the activity.

Sentence Show

Divide the class into groups of three, and give each group a sheet of writing paper, a sheet of white construction paper, and crayons or markers. Ask each group to write a three-part sentence that describes "who is doing what" and "where." Have them work together to draw on construction paper a large picture of the person or thing that the sentence is about. Invite a group to stand in front of the class and present the parts of their sentence: ask the first person to silently hold up the "who" picture, the second person to pantomime the action (i.e., "doing what") of the sentence, and the third person to spell out the word that describes "where." Have the rest of the class write down what they think the sentence is, based on the clues given. Invite students to share their predictions, and then have the group say their sentence aloud. Repeat the process with other groups.

Materials

- writing paper
- white construction paper
- crayons or markers

Objectives

- Write three-part sentences.
- Illustrate, pantomime, and spell out parts of a sentence.

Variation: Invite the third person of the group to use American Sign Language letters to spell out the word that describes "where."

Extension: Invite groups to illustrate and pantomime parts of a story they've written.

More Scrambled Sentences

In advance, make sets of picture/word cards by following the same procedure used in the Scrambled Sentences activity (see page 36), except compose three-part sentences that describe "where" as well as "who is doing what" (e.g., *The monkey at the zoo climbs a tree*). Remove the "connector cards" from each set, and place them in random order on the ledge of the chalkboard (or attach them to the chalkboard using tape, removable tack-up, or flat magnets). Give each student a sheet of writing paper. Place in a pocket chart one set of picture cards, and have students read aloud the corresponding labels. Ask students to identify the connector words needed to complete a sentence. Invite a volunteer to remove the required word cards from the chalkboard ledge and place them with the picture cards in proper sequence to form a sentence. Ask the class to read the sentence aloud and then write it on their paper. Repeat the process with additional sets of picture cards.

Materials

- "Who," "Doing What," and "Where" Picture Cards (pages 78–88)
- Sample Picture-Card Sentences sheet (page 89)
- index cards
- marker
- erasable crayons
- large envelopes
- chalkboard and chalk
- tape, removable tack-up, or flat magnets (optional)
- writing paper
- pocket chart

Objectives

- Compose three-part sentences.
- Select appropriate "connector words" to complete pictorial sentences.

Variation: Teach this activity to small groups. Attach flat magnets to the backs of all the picture and word cards. Invite students to manipulate the cards on a magnetic surface (e.g., a chalkboard, a metal filing cabinet, a lap board) to form sentences.

Extension: Invite partners or small groups to complete the activity independently.

Lights, Camera, Action!

For each student, photocopy the Filmstrip Pattern sheet onto a piece of construction paper. Cut the slits, as indicated, and staple on the bottom half of the page a stack of copy-paper strips for students to write on. Give each student one of the filmstrip sheets, a sentence strip, and a ruler. Have students draw a vertical line on their sentence strip every 3" (7 cm) to divide the strip into five "picture frames." Then invite them to draw "who," "doing what" and "where" pictures inside the three middle picture frames, leaving the two on the ends of the strip blank. Show students how to pull their illustrated strip through the "projector" (the slits) to view their pictures, frame by frame. Ask students to write one or more corresponding three-part sentences on the attached paper strips (one sentence per strip). Invite students to share their "filmstrips" and sentences.

Materials

- Filmstrip Pattern sheet (page 92)
- construction paper
- scissors (or cutting board) and stapler
- 3" x 10" (8 cm x 30 cm) white copy-paper strips
- 3" x 15" (8 cm x 38 cm) sentence-strip pieces
- rulers
- crayons or markers

Objectives

- Draw pictures that represent the "who," "doing what," and "where" parts of a sentence.
- Write a three-part sentence that corresponds to illustrations.

Extension: Have students make several filmstrips and write a corresponding sentence for each one. Invite partners to exchange their creations and randomly select one of the filmstrips to view. Have them identify the matching sentence among those written.

Cinquains, Anyone?

In advance, make a transparency of the Cinquains sheet. On the chalkboard, write the headings *Naming Words, Describing Words,* and *Doing Words.* Invite students to brainstorm words and tell you the correct chalkboard heading to write them under. Then display the Cinquain sheet on an overhead projector, and have the class read the sample poems aloud. Explain that cinquains are special poems that include "naming," "describing," and "doing" words like those written on the chalkboard. Have students classify the words used in the poems. Then invite them to use the cinquain format to write their own descriptive poems.

Materials

- Cinquains sheet (page 93)
- overhead projector and transparency
- chalkboard and chalk

Objectives

- Categorize words as "naming," "describing," and "doing."
- Identify nouns, adjectives, and verbs in a cinquain.
- Collaborate with others to write cinquains.

Cinquain
——————

Ryan
Handsome, happy
Swimming, running, drawing
Makes people laugh
Ryan

Variation: For more advanced learners, use the formal labels *noun, adjective,* and *verb* instead of "naming," "describing," and "doing."

Extension: Invite partners to write and illustrate a cinquain for a particular theme, such as an upcoming holiday, a science lesson, or a favorite hobby.

Questions and Answers

In advance, write each incomplete sentence from the Questions and Answers sheet on separate sentence strips and laminate the strips. Write the following questions on chart paper or poster board: *What object do you have? What is its size? What is its shape? What is its color? What can it do? What can't it do? Why do you like it?*

Explain to students that it's possible to create a story by answering some simple questions. To demonstrate, first have the class decide on a favorite object (e.g., a toy, an animal). Then display the chart and read aloud each question. Invite students to brainstorm possible answers. Use a dry-erase marker or an erasable crayon to write some of the students' answers on the laminated strips to complete the sentences. Place the sentences in proper sequence in a pocket chart, and invite the class to read aloud the story they've helped create.

Materials

- Questions and Answers sheet (page 94)
- marker
- sentence strips
- chart paper or poster board
- dry-erase marker or erasable crayon
- pocket chart

Objectives

- Use inquiry to help decide a story's contents.
- Select nouns, adjectives, and verbs to complete a story.

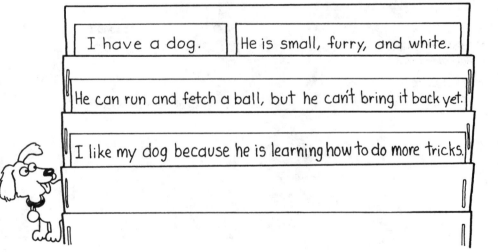

Variation: Invite pairs of students to write their own descriptive stories on photocopies of the Questions and Answers sheet. Have partners take turns asking each other the questions and recording the answers. Then invite students to read aloud their stories to the rest of the class.

Extension: Use fill-in-the-blank stories to help reinforce parts of speech. Prompt students by asking for a particular kind of word—e.g., a noun, an adjective, or a verb. Be sure to explain that nouns are "naming" words, adjectives are "describing" words, and verbs are "doing" words. (Note: Depending on the skill level of your students, you may wish to include adverbs in the lesson.)

Meet Mr. Story Face

In advance, photocopy the Mr. Story Face sheet for students. Make an enlarged version of the reproducible, and post it in front of the class. Introduce "Mr. Story Face," explaining that he helps students write stories. Invite the class to choose an animal (real or imaginary) to write about. Demonstrate how to use the visual cues in the illustrated face to think of story details. Pretend to be Mr. Story Face as you prompt students for answers to the following questions:

Materials

- Mr. Story Face sheet (page 95)
- chalkboard and chalk
- crayons or markers

Objectives

- Organize and structure the parts of a story.
- Think about and write a descriptive story that includes five related ideas.

▲ *Who is your story about?*
   (Point to the speech bubble.)

▲ *What does he or she look like?*
   (Point to the word *look*—Mr. Story Face's eyes and ears.)

▲ *What special qualities does he or she have?*
   (Point to the word *have* below Mr. Story Face's nose.)

▲ *What does he or she like to do?*
   (Point to the word *do* below Mr. Story Face's mouth.)

▲ *Why does he or she like to do it?*
   (Point to the letter *y* that is part of Mr. Story Face's shirt.)

Use students' responses to write on the chalkboard the sentences of a story. Give each student crayons or markers and a photocopy of the Mr. Story Face sheet. As you read aloud the class story, ask students to color in the Mr. Story Face's feature that corresponds to the part of the story being read. For example, students color in Mr. Story Face's eyes when they hear you read a sentence that describes the character's looks.

Variation: Have students (or partners) write their own answers to the questions. Then demonstrate how to connect and rewrite the answers to compose a story.

48

Story Swap

In advance, photocopy the Story Frames sheets, and cut apart the three story frames on each page. Guide students through the writing process by writing one of the story frames on the chalkboard and having students complete the story as a group. After guided instruction, divide the class into partners (or groups of three), and give each pair of students a story frame. Have partners work together to fill in the first blank of the story. Then ask students to exchange papers and complete the next portion of the new story they receive. Repeat the process until the story frames are complete. Invite volunteers to read aloud the collaborative stories.

Materials

- Story Frames sheets (pages 96–98)
- scissors
- chalkboard and chalk

Objectives

- Develop a story by completing a cloze activity.
- Select words that are appropriate for a specific theme.

Variation: Laminate the story-frame sheets, and use dry-erase markers to fill in the blanks to create simple, nondescriptive sentences. Have partners rewrite the sentences to be more descriptive and complete. Invite volunteers to read aloud the "new and improved" stories.

Extension: Invite students to partner up with older students in another class and write additional story frames for others to complete. For extra fun, invite partners to draw picture prompts to go along with their incomplete stories.

It's All in the Picture

In advance, collect action-oriented pictures from wordless books and children's magazines. Label five index cards *Who, Doing What, Where, When,* and *Why.* Explain to the class that pictures often "tell" stories. Display one of the pictures, and invite students to use clues in the illustration or photograph to "pre-think" a story—to describe everything they can about the picture. Ask them to "look beyond the picture" and predict what the individual is thinking and feeling, what may have already occurred, and what might happen next. Encourage interpretation, prediction, analysis, and problem-solving. After the picture has been thoroughly discussed, tape the index cards onto the chalkboard. Explain that determining "who," "doing what," "where," "when," and "why" can help identify and organize important parts of a story. Invite a volunteer to select one of the story elements (e.g., "where") and relate it to the picture. Under the appropriate index card, write down one or two words to summarize what was said. For example, write the word *beach* below the label *Where* to summarize the sentence *It was a warm, sunny day at the beach.* Continue the process until all five story elements have been identified, and then have the class use the information to develop an oral story.

Materials

- assorted pictures
- index cards
- marker
- tape
- chalkboard and chalk

Objectives

- Describe pictures in terms of "who," "doing what," "where," "when," and "why."
- Interpret pictures to help develop an oral story.

Variation: Divide the class into five small groups, and assign each group a different part of a story (for example, one group describes "who"). After five minutes to share and pool ideas, ask representatives from each group to explain "who," "doing what," "where," "when," and "why" to create an entertaining, collaborative story.

Extension: Have students write stories that correspond to picture prompts. For added fun, invite students to draw pictures for partners to write about.

Elastic Sentences

In advance, make an enlarged, laminated photocopy of the Stretch It! sheet to post on the chalk tray or an easel. Begin the lesson by reading aloud, in a monotone voice, a few simple sentences (e.g., *The dog barked* and *The ball bounced*). Have students vote on whether they thought the sentences were exciting to listen to. Explain that good writers stretch out sentences and make them "come alive" by using special words, exciting ideas, and intriguing plots. Use a dry-erase marker or an erasable crayon to write one of the simple sentences under the "who" and "doing what" labels on the laminated chart. Have students brainstorm "when," "where," and "why" words as you write their ideas under the appropriate headings. List additional describing words to add to the sentence, such as *big, brown,* and *loudly.* Hold up a large rubber band for students to see as you reread the simple sentence. Read it again, but this time include one of the details written on the Stretch It! chart. As you recite the expanded sentence, stretch the rubber band. Continue to stretch the rubber band as you add more and more descriptive details to the sentence. For example, *The big, brown dog barked loudly in the morning because he was hungry.* Repeat the process with a new simple sentence, this time having students say aloud expanded sentences as you stretch the rubber band.

Materials

- Stretch It! sheet (page 99)
- a list of simple subject/verb sentences
- dry-erase marker or erasable crayon
- easel or chalkboard chalk tray
- large rubber band

Objectives

- Expand simple sentences to include words that describe "when," "where," and "why."
- Compare the information and the "excitement" of simple sentences to those that include more detail.

Extension: Make a photocopy of the Stretch It! sheet for each student to fill in as you write the words and sentences on the enlarged version. For a greater challenge, write a simple sentence on the chalkboard, and invite individual students or partners to complete their Stretch It! sheet independently. Then invite volunteers to read aloud their expanded sentence.

Peek-a-Boo Stories

In advance, photocopy a Peek-a-Boo Story sheet for each student. Show students how to fold the sheet to make a miniature book: Fold the sheet in half on the solid line, and then fold in the sides on the dotted lines so that the "when" section is on top (use the numbers as a guide). Explain to the class that they are to "prethink" a story by illustrating the five story elements—"when," "where," "who," "doing what," and "why"—in their book. Assist students in selecting a topic by brainstorming and listing on the chalkboard some story ideas. Invite each student to draw in his or her book some pictures that represent the different story elements. Divide the class into pairs, and have partners take turns sharing the story they've illustrated. After they describe the story orally, help students write a detailed sentence or story (depending on the ability level of the students) that corresponds to the pictures in their Peek-a-Boo book.

Materials

- Peek-a-Boo Story sheet (page 100)
- crayons or markers

Objectives

- Draw illustrations to represent the five elements of a story (i.e., "when," "where," "who," "doing what," and "why").
- Write a detailed sentence or story that corresponds to pictures in the Peek-a-Boo book.

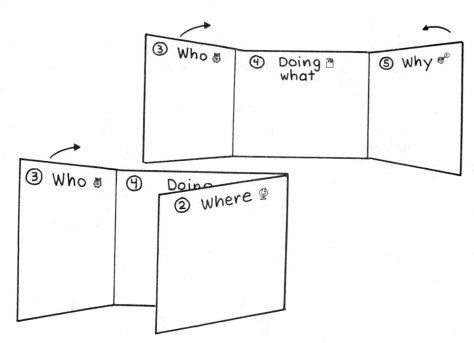

Variation: Draw writing lines on the back of the Peek-a-Boo Story sheet before making photocopies. Have students open up their book and write the descriptive sentence or story on the back.

Extension: Instead of drawing pictures, have students write each section of the story on the appropriate section of the Peek-a-Boo book. Invite volunteers to share their story, one part at a time, while the rest of the class predicts what's going to happen next.

Connect a Story

In advance, make a transparency of the Connect a Story sheet. Decide on a story theme, and then draw inside the boxes illustrations that represent "when," "where," "who," "doing what," and "why." Display the transparency on an overhead projector, and ask students to look at each picture. Explain that the illustrations represent different parts of a story. Ask the class to identify which picture represents "when," and then write the word *when* above the picture. Repeat the process with the "where," "who," "doing what," and "why" pictures. On the lines below the pictures, have students help you write a corresponding story, deciding together the story sequence. As you write the story, draw lines from one picture to the next to show the order of events.

Materials

- Connect a Story sheet (page 101)
- overhead projector, transparency, and markers

Objectives

- Illustrate and organize the parts of a story.
- Add details to expand a sentence into a story.
- Combine related ideas to write a story.

Variation: Have volunteers help decide which pictures to draw in each box. Show more than one way to connect the boxes so students see how the story sequence can vary.

Extension: Write different parts of a scrambled story in the five boxes, and make photocopies of the sheet for the class. Have students draw lines from one box to the next to show the sequence of events. Then have them rewrite the story to match the indicated sequence. Invite students to share and compare the stories they've written.

Read My Mind

In advance, enlarge and laminate the Read My Mind sheet. In the thought bubble, draw with a dry-erase marker a picture of an object (or tape a picture of an object in the bubble). Conceal the picture with a stick-on note or a piece of paper. Give each student a photocopy of the Read My Mind sheet, and post the laminated chart in front of the classroom. Explain to students that they are to use clues to "read your mind" and identify the picture hidden on the chart. Begin by writing on the chart three words that describe the mystery object. Have the class copy and read aloud the words. Continue offering "clues" by filling in the answers to the questions on the chart as they relate to the hidden picture. Once again, have students copy and read aloud the written information. When the chart is filled in, invite students to "read your mind" and identify the object. Then uncover the picture so that students may see if they guessed correctly. Conclude the lesson by using the information listed on the chart to write a sentence that describes the object. Have students copy the sentence or write one of their own. (Ask more advanced learners to expand the sentence into a story.) For extra fun, invite students to draw pictures of the object in their photocopied thought bubble.

Materials

- Read My Mind sheet (page 102)
- dry-erase marker
- tape and small magazine pictures of objects (optional)
- stick-on notes or paper
- crayons or markers (optional)

Objectives

- Write descriptive words and sentences about a "mystery" object.
- Identify the "who," "doing what," "where," and "when" in a sentence or story.
- Collect and combine information to write descriptive sentences.

Variation: Divide the class into pairs. Give each student a photocopy of the Read My Mind sheet. Have one student in each pair choose a small object to hide in his or her hand or lap. Ask partners to pose the questions from the Read My Mind sheet, write the answers they are told, and then identify the mystery object. Have student pairs decide together the corresponding sentence to write. Then invite partners to switch roles.

Sentence Builders

In advance, make photocopies of the Sentence Builder sheet for students. Make a transparency of the sheet and display it on an overhead projector. Write on the chalkboard some color words, size and shape words, and "texture" words (e.g., *rough, smooth, bumpy*). Give each student some crayons and a photocopy of the Sentence Builder sheet. As a group, read the words at the top of each blank box. Explain to students that they are to preplan a sentence by drawing appropriate pictures in the boxes. Show them an example by drawing the following pictures on the transparency: a sunset *(When)*, a bunny *(Who)*, a stick figure hiding an egg behind a bush *(Is Doing What)*, a backyard *(Where)*, and a stick figure eyeing a small object on the ground *(Why)*. Have students help you think of a corresponding sentence to write on the lines below the pictures. Read aloud the "describing words" listed on the chalkboard, and encourage volunteers to suggest sentences that include a few of the words. Write one of their suggestions on the lines. For example, *Early one morning, a white bunny was hiding colored eggs in my backyard for me to find.* Point out "connector words" needed to complete the sentence. Then have students complete their own Sentence Builder sheet. Invite volunteers to share their pictures and read their sentence aloud.

Materials

- Sentence Builder sheet (page 103)
- overhead projector, transparency, and markers
- chalkboard and chalk
- crayons

Objectives

- Illustrate an expanded sentence that describes "who," "doing what," "when," "where," and "why."
- Add adjectives to a sentence to make it more descriptive.

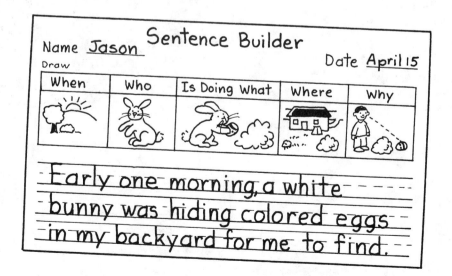

Extension: Invite more advanced learners to write a corresponding story to go along with their preplanned pictures.

Story Ladders

This activity is best introduced after a special event, such as a field trip or a class party. In advance, make a photocopy of the Short Story Ladder for each student. Make a transparency of the ladder, and display it on an overhead projector alongside a blank (or lined) transparency sheet. Explain to the class that the "story ladder" is going to help them organize and keep track of the parts in a story. Review with students what happened at the special event. As you color in the first rung of the ladder, have students repeat what happened first. Put a checkmark by the word *First* below the first rung. Then write a corresponding sentence on the blank transparency. Continue the process with the rest of the story, checking off the transition words *Then, Next,* and *Finally* as you complete the narrative story. Distribute writing paper and a photocopy of the Short Story Ladder to each student. Invite students to color in and check off each rung as they write their own sequential story.

Materials

- Story Ladders sheet (page 104)
- overhead projector, transparencies, and markers
- writing paper
- crayons or markers

Objectives

- Write a narrative story that includes a definite sequence of events.
- Identify and use transition words that indicate passage of time.

Variation: Cut the climber from the ladder, and make separate transparencies of the two parts. As you narrate the steps of the story, show the climber moving up the ladder.

Extension: Invite more advanced learners to use the Super Story Ladder to write an expanded version of the story. Explain that the extra rungs of the ladder represent additional descriptive sentences to add to each part of the story. Demonstrate how to write an expanded story before having students work independently.

Story Walk

This is an ongoing activity that initially requires plenty of guided and collaborative practice. Its generic format enables it to be used for a variety of writing topics, including factual events, personal narratives, autobiographical information, and fictional stories. In advance, make an enlarged 3-D version of the Story Walk graphic by gluing a photocopy onto poster board and then adding paper footprints and a yarn pathway. Post the chart on the wall in front of the class for easy reference. Use the rebus pictures on the chart to "walk" students through the basic steps of story development: identify who or what the story is about (the talk bubble), describe what happens (the des-"cry"-be prompt next to the "what" wrapped present), identify what the main character does to solve the issue or problem (the *d* + the ghostly *"oo"*), and explain why the character does the action (the *y* symbol). Practice the Story Walk procedure several times with collaborative oral stories before progressing students into independent writing. After students become familiar with the process, distribute photocopies of the Story Walk sheet for students to use each time they write a story. Have them color in the footprints as they complete each step of the pathway. Whenever students read aloud stories they've written, point to the Story Walk graphic that indicates which step is being discussed. Invite students to sing the following song to the tune of "Daddy's Taking Us to the Zoo Tomorrow" or "London Bridge" (or any other appropriate melody).

Materials

- Story Walk sheet (page 105)
- craft items (poster board, yarn, construction paper, scissors, glue)

Objectives

- Identify and describe the "who," "doing what," and "why" of a story.
- Write an informational story using the three-part Story Walk format.

*I'm going on a story walk, story walk, story walk,
I'm going on a story walk . . . I'm gonna write a story!
First I tell what it's about, what it's about, what it's about,
First I tell what it's about . . . as I write my story!*

(Repeat three more times: "Then I describe what happens . . .," "Then I tell what to do . . .," and "Then I tell why it happened . . . .")

Story Stumpers

In advance, review the questions on the Story Stumpers sheet. Introduce the activity before a designated story-sharing time. Tell the students that they are to listen very carefully to each story because you are going to ask some questions to try and stump them. Invite a volunteer to read aloud his or her story. As the story is being read, mentally note a few related questions to ask. After the story is read, begin asking the "stumper questions." Invite the volunteer to select classmates to provide the answers, allowing two tries per question. List on the chalkboard the questions that stump students. As a class, review and discuss the answers, identifying which information was included in the story and which information was not. Repeat the process with another student's story. For a special treat, pin Good Listening! badges on students at the end of the activity.

Materials

- Story Stumpers sheet and Good Listening! badges (page 106)
- students' stories
- chalkboard and chalk
- safety pins

Objectives

- Identify important details of a story by answering questions.
- Reinforce critical thinking skills by listening to and reading aloud stories.
- Strengthen the link between reading and writing to improve overall literacy.

Extension: Before sharing stories aloud, invite students to write their own "stumper questions" to ask their classmates. (You may choose to enlarge and post the Story Stumpers sheet as a guide.)

Story Outlines

Write the following prompts on an overhead transparency, leaving space between each one: *Who is your story about? What problem or event happened? What did the character do? Why did the character do it?* Tell the class that they are going to help you put together a story by answering the given questions. Emphasize the importance of prewriting—outlining the main parts of a story in advance. Invite students to suggest three or four different answers for each question, and write each idea on a separate index card. Sort the cards according to which question they answer. Invite a volunteer to select a card from each category, and copy the selected answers onto the transparency. Have the class read aloud the parts of the story you've written. Brainstorm additional details to add to the story to make it more complete. Write the expanded story on another transparency. Then invite the class to read aloud the story they helped create.

Materials

- overhead projector, transparencies, and marker
- large index cards

Objectives

- Outline the main elements of a story.
- Add details to make a story more complete.
- Compose and share aloud a story.

A baby pelican

There was a big fire.

He asked friends for help.

Hero

He didn't want people to get hurt.

Variation: As a warm-up activity, have the class use a familiar story to answer the four questions. Invite students to retell the story as you write down the relevant information on the transparency.

Extension: Have each student (or pair of students) write on separate index cards creative answers to the questions. Collect the cards and sort them into the four categories. Invite each student to select a card from each category and use the information to write his or her own story.

Sentence Starters

In advance, write the following sentence starters on sentence strips and then laminate the strips for repetitive use. (Leave plenty of space for the blanks.)

Since it was _____, I _____.
He was _____, but he _____.
She not only _____, but she also _____.
It was _____, but _____.
She was _____ and _____, however _____.
It was unusual for it _____, but _____.
Although it was _____, it was _____.
I will _____, but meanwhile _____.

Materials

- sentence strips
- pocket chart
- dry-erase marker

Objectives

- Combine ideas to form compound and complex sentences.
- Complete cloze phrases to create multiple-idea sentences.

Display the sentence strips in a pocket chart, and read the first incomplete sentence aloud. Have students suggest words and phrases to fill in the blanks, and use a dry-erase marker to write one of the suggestions on the sentence strip. Remind the class that good writers use exciting vocabulary along with creative ideas to make their writing "come alive." Continue the process with the rest of the sentences. Encourage multiple responses by inviting students to erase and replace words to form new sentences.

Since it was raining, I got wet.

Variation: Write nouns, verbs, and adjectives on separate index cards for students to place inside the pocket chart to complete the sentences. Or use corresponding picture prompts to help students complete the sentences.

Extension: Use the sentence-starter format to develop a collaborative story. Sit with students in a circle. Begin a story by saying aloud an incomplete sentence. For example, *Once upon a time, there was a _____ dragon.* Ask the student sitting to your right to complete the sentence and then add another sentence starter. Have the next person in the circle repeat the process. Continue building the story until each student has had a turn.

Dinosaur Details

In advance, photocopy the Dinosaur Details sheet for students. Make a transparency of the sheet, and display it on an overhead projector. Copy a descriptive story or passage onto chart paper. Explain to the class that the dinosaur is going to help them discover details in a story. Read aloud the preselected story. Then reread it, and have students raise their hands each time they hear a new detail. Invite a volunteer to use a colored pencil to underline each corresponding sentence on the chart paper. For each detail students identify, draw a spike on the dinosaur picture. When finished, have the class help summarize the highlighted details. Invite students to count the number of spikes on the dinosaur to determine how many details were included in the story. Then distribute photocopies of the Dinosaur Details sheet. Invite individuals or partners to use colored pencils and their own prewritten stories to highlight details and add corresponding dinosaur spikes.

Materials

- Dinosaur Details sheet (page 107)
- overhead projector, transparency, and markers
- short story or passage that includes many details
- chart paper
- colored pencils
- students' stories

Objectives

- Identify and summarize supporting details in a story.
- Highlight and count the number of details in a prewritten story.

Variation: Have each student hold up a letter *d* card or a miniature dinosaur picture each time they hear a detail being read aloud.

Extension: Have students write a word or phrase inside each spike to summarize the corresponding detail.

Digging for Details

In advance, make a transparency of the Digging for Details sheet, and display it on an overhead projector. Make photocopies of the sheet, and distribute one to each student. Write on the chalkboard the following simple story: *I went to a birthday party. It was fun. I went home.* Have the class read the sentences aloud. Invite a volunteer to explain why the story is not interesting: It does not have enough details. Explain to the class that details are needed to make a story exciting and inviting to read—that these vivid words help readers "see in their mind" a picture of the events taking place. Divide the class into partners or small groups, and have students "dig in their memory banks" for details to add to the story. Ask them to think of birthday parties they have attended, heard about, read about, or would like to have. List a couple of details (in short phrases) on the chalkboard to guide students as they write their ideas on their Digging for Details sheet. After five or ten minutes, invite students to share some of the details they have "discovered." Summarize and write their suggestions on the Digging for Details transparency. As a class, revise and rewrite the story to include the details listed.

Materials

- Digging for Details sheet (page 108)
- overhead projector, transparency, and marker
- chalkboard and chalk

Objectives

- Identify details to add to a story.
- Revise a story to include more details.

Extension: Divide the class into pairs, and ask each student to fill out a Digging for Details sheet in response to his or her partner's story (written during a previous lesson). Invite pairs to work together to revise and rewrite the stories. Be sure to recognize and reward partners for good cooperation and teamwork.

Super Story Walk

Teach this activity only after students have sufficiently practiced the Story Walk format (see page 57). In advance, use poster board or chart paper to make an enlarged, 3-D version of the Super Story Walk sheet to post in the classroom for easy reference. Review with students how to "take a story walk." Compare the steps of the Story Walk format to the expanded sequence of Super Story Walk. Identify the additional elements on the more advanced chart: the title, the setting (the globe), the moral or lesson to learn (the symbol *y*), and the personal opinion (the thought bubble). Use the following generic prompts to guide students through the process:

Materials

- Super Story Walk sheet (page 109)
- poster board or chart paper
- Story Walk chart (see activity, page 57)

Objectives

- Use the Super Story Walk guidelines to organize and develop stories.
- Write a story that explains "who," "doing what," "when," "where," "how," and "why."

When taking a story walk . . .
   What is the title of your story?
   Who or what is the story about?
   Where and when does the story take place?
   What happens (describe the problem or event)?
   What does the character do? Why does the character do it?
   What does the character think or feel about what happened?

(Note that for nonfiction writing, the prompts are slightly different: *What is the title of your story?, Who or what is the story about?, Where and when does the story take place?, What does the character do, or what can the object do?, Why is the character or object important?,* and *What do you think about the character or object?*) After students have had several opportunities to compare collaborative stories, have them use the Super Story Walk format to write stories independently or with a partner.

Extension: Distribute photocopies of the Super Story Walk sheet, and have students color in the footprints as they complete each step of the story-writing process.

Oh, P-L-E-A-S-E!

In advance, make a transparency of the My Best Friend story, and write the word *persuade* on the chalkboard. Define the word for the class, giving examples that are relevant to the age level of the students. To check for understanding, invite students to persuade you to grant extra time for recess. Explain that they must give you reasons to prove their point. List the students' ideas on the chalkboard as they share them aloud. As a group, decide which reasons are the most persuasive, and then erase the other suggestions. Have the class use the listed information to help you orally compose a persuasive story about the length of recess. Once students understand the art of persuasion, display the My Best Friend story on the overhead projector. Read it together, and highlight all the good points about owning a dog. Then ask students (individuals or partners) to use the information in the story to help write a persuasive letter to their parents about getting a dog. To guide instruction, write on the chalkboard a poor example of a persuasive letter for students to modify. At the end of the activity, invite students to share their persuasive letters with the rest of the class.

Materials

- My Best Friend story (page 110)
- overhead projector, transparency, and marker
- chalkboard and chalk
- writing paper

Objectives

- Develop a persuasive argument.
- Write a persuasive letter by using information from a descriptive story.

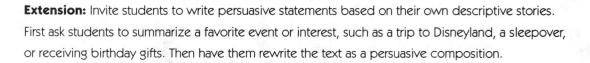

Why we should get longer recess:
1. We'll get extra energy to study.
2. More exercise is healthy.
3. We'll work harder in class to earn more recess.

Extension: Invite students to write persuasive statements based on their own descriptive stories. First ask students to summarize a favorite event or interest, such as a trip to Disneyland, a sleepover, or receiving birthday gifts. Then have them rewrite the text as a persuasive composition.

Story Snake

In advance, enlarge the Story Snake sheet, and glue it onto chart paper or poster board. Review with the class the plot of a selected story. Explain that stories often revolve around solving a problem. Show the class the Story Snake graphic, and tell them that it is a "special snake" that helps solve problems. Give an example of conflict resolution from the selected story. As each part of the example is stated, point to the related word on the Story Snake graphic. For example, *Cinderella ("somebody") wished that she could go to the ball ("somewhere"), but her mean old stepmother said no ("something"). So the fairy godmother granted Cinderella's wish ("so then").* Expand the discussion to include problem-solving in everyday life. Invite volunteers to share experiences in which they had to solve a problem. Select one of the examples to expand into a conflict-resolution story. Have the class help guide you through the Story Snake steps to orally compose the story.

Materials

- Story Snake sheet (page 111)
- chart paper or poster board and glue
- short story that focuses on problem-solving (e.g., Cinderella)

Objectives

- Develop and practice skills in resolution writing.
- Compose oral stories that pertain to problem-solving and conflict resolution.

Extension: Ask students to independently (or with partners) write problem-solving stories. Encourage them to refer to the Story Snake graphic. Be sure to recognize and reward students for using good problem-solving techniques.

He Said, She Said

In advance, write simple questions on separate index cards (e.g., *What is your favorite color?*, *What time do you go to bed?*). Distribute the cards to volunteers. Have one of the students read aloud and answer his or her question. Ask the rest of the class to identify who was speaking. Point out to the class that they were able to identify who was speaking because they could see the individual; but with writing, one cannot see the person talking. Explain that the author of a story uses special "talk marks" called *quotation marks* to let the reader know when someone is talking (use your first two fingers on each hand to demonstrate what talk marks look like). Write on a sentence strip the volunteer's answer in the form of a quoted statement, but leave off the punctuation. For example, *Ryan said My favorite color is blue.* Place the sentence strip in the top row of a pocket chart. Then have students identify where in the sentence the volunteer started speaking. Place two clothespins on each side of the quoted text to mark where the quotation marks should be written. Add the comma that precedes the opening quote, and explain that this special mark means "pause and give the person a chance to talk." Have students read the sentence, pausing before the quoted statement. Repeat the process with the other prewritten questions, inviting volunteers to add the "clothespin quotes." Finish the lesson by reading together the pocket-chart strips and inviting students to use their fingers to indicate where the talk marks are inserted.

Materials

- index cards
- marker
- sentence strips
- pocket chart
- clothespins

Objectives

- Learn how to write and punctuate quoted text.
- Correct written dialogue to include proper punctuation.

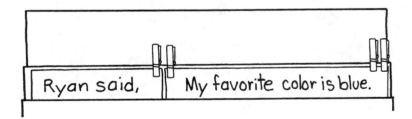

Variation: After guided instruction, give partners a laminated sentence strip, a dry-erase marker or an erasable crayon, and four clothespins. Have one student in each pair write on the sentence strip an unpunctuated quote for his or her partner to mark with clothespins.

Extension: Distribute photocopies of a dialogue-rich passage in which the quotation marks have been omitted. Invite students to read the passage and use colored pencils to insert the proper punctuation.

What Did You Say?

In advance, copy the following incomplete story onto a transparency. Leave plenty of space to write the missing words.

Materials

• overhead projector, transparency, and marker

Objectives

• Add words to complete written dialogue.
• Write a narrative story that includes dialogue between two characters.

Joey woke up early. He was too excited to sleep. Today was his mother's birthday and he had a special surprise. He jumped out of bed and ran to find his mother in the kitchen.
When he saw her, he said, _____.
Joey's mother smiled. She said, _____.
Then he said, _____.
With a twinkle in her eye, Joey's mother asked, _____.
Joey answered, _____.

Display the story on an overhead projector, and read it aloud. Explain to students that they are to supply the missing words to complete the conversation between Joey and his mother. Reread the story, stopping before each missing statement. Have students brainstorm possible responses and decide together which suggestions to use to complete the passage. After all the responses have been written in, read the complete story together. For extra fun, read aloud the introduction, and then invite the girls to read the part of the mother and the boys to read the part of Joey.

"Grandma, what big teeth you have!"

Variation: Give each student a photocopy of the incomplete dialogue to complete independently or with a partner. Invite students to read aloud and compare their story.

Extension: Invite partners to write stories that contain dialogue. For extra motivation, have them write a story based on a personal experience (e.g., a discussion they had with the next-door neighbor) or their favorite television or storybook characters. For extra fun, provide students with cartoon strips in which the dialogue has been omitted, and invite students to fill in the missing text.

Think It Through

This is an ongoing activity that requires substantial modeling, prompting, and guided practice. In advance, use yellow construction paper and scissors to make smiley-face lightbulbs, and write the phrase *Good Thinking!* at the bottom of each bulb. Use poster board to make a chart that includes the following prompts and examples:

Materials

- yellow construction paper
- scissors
- markers
- poster board

Objectives

- Form an opinion based on the content of a story.
- Use prompts to help incorporate interpretation, prediction, and analysis into writing.

- I know . . . . I wonder if . . . .
  Example: *I know that Cinderella's stepsisters were surprised when the slipper fit on Cinderella's foot. I wonder if they will really be nice to her when they live together in the palace.*

- The important thing about . . . is . . . .
  Example: *The important thing about Cinderella is that she was kind and helpful to her family even when they were mean to her.*

- Fortunately . . . . Unfortunately . . . .
  Example: *Fortunately Cinderella was nice. Unfortunately her stepmother and stepsisters were mean.*

- I think the author wanted me to know . . . because . . . .
  Example: *I think the author wanted me to know that good wins out over evil because Cinderella and the Prince found each other in the end.*

Discuss with students the importance of writing with a purpose. Explain that many authors write to state an opinion, share knowledge, or teach a lesson. Read aloud the prompts and the examples written on the chart. Select other favorite stories to retell, and invite students to use the prompts as they summarize, analyze, and interpret each plot. Use the paper lightbulbs to reward good thinking.

Extension: Have students or partners use the prompts to help analyze their own writing.

Performance Checkoff: Emergent and Early Writers

Student's Name _____	Date	Comments
Conveys ideas using pictures or symbols		
Writes from left to right		
Includes initial consonants		
Spells words based on initial and ending sounds		
Reads and shares own writing		
Includes some middle sounds when spelling words		
Writes using whole words		
Uses spaces between words		
Writes simple sentences that make sense		
Uses capital letters and periods		
Expands sentences to include three or more elements		
Writes multiple sentences that share a common theme		
Stays focused on the topic		
Writes sentences that include a beginning, a middle, and an end		
Organizes story ideas in logical sequence		

Teaching Beginning Writing © 1999 Creative Teaching Press

Performance Checkoff:
Developing and Established Writers

Student's Name _____	Date	Comments
Includes a title		
Organizes story ideas in logical sequence		
Uses supporting details		
Stays focused on the topic		
Writes sentences and stories that have a clear beginning, middle, and end		
Varies the length of sentences		
Varies the way sentences begin		
Uses literary devices (metaphor/simile)		
Writes in paragraph form		
Writes descriptive stories		
Writes narrative stories		
Writes persuasive stories		
Writes informational passages		
Revises to strengthen content		
Edits for punctuation, grammar, and spelling		

Teaching Beginning Writing © 1999 Creative Teaching Press

Story Log

Name _____

Date _____

Characters	Setting

1	2	3

Story Endings

1. Now that it is all over, everybody laughed . . . even the monster!

2. After that, the magic wand never worked again.

3. But when they got back, no one would believe what happened.

4. Then the giant bellowed, "Maybe it isn't so bad being a giant after all!"

5. Then the greedy, little leprechaun took the pot of gold and was never seen again.

6. The crusty old pirate left the deserted island, but he knew he would be back some day.

7. From that day forward, the little boy never felt lonely again.

8. No one was afraid of the fire-breathing dragon again.

9. And then the scary, little witch flew off on her broomstick, but we knew she'd be back next Halloween.

10. Closing her eyes to make a wish, the excited little girl knew that her wish had already come true.

11. He ran as fast as he could, hoping he would never see anything like that again.

12. And that was one secret that she knew she would never tell.

Teaching Beginning Writing © 1999 Creative Teaching Press

In the Beginning

1. In the beginning, all of the boys and girls were happy and excited because _____

_____.

But then, _____

_____.

Now _____

_____.

- -

2. In the beginning, the stingy, old king kept all of the gold for himself because _____

_____.

But then, _____

_____.

Now _____

_____.

- -

3. In the beginning, the mean, old witch loved to scare anybody she could because _____

_____.

But then, _____

_____.

Now _____

_____.

- -

4. In the beginning, the grumpy, old giant just growled and snarled because _____

_____.

But then, _____

_____.

Now _____

_____.

In the Beginning

5. In the beginning, the playful, little elf played jokes on everyone because _____

_____.

But then, _____

_____.

Now _____

_____.

- -

6. In the beginning, we didn't think that it would be any fun at all because _____

_____.

But then, _____

_____.

Now _____

_____.

- -

7. In the beginning, they were too scared to go into the haunted house because _____

_____.

But then, _____

_____.

Now _____

_____.

- -

8. In the beginning, the little, white polar bear just sat at the edge because _____

_____.

But then, _____

_____.

Now _____

_____.

Story Detectives

1. They went back home and lived happily ever after.

2. The next day, the little puppy began to look all around for his bone, but he still couldn't find it.

3. It was almost Valentine's Day, and Mama Bunny was baking special heart-shaped cookies.

4. But they still had to find the perfect Christmas tree to take home.

5. It had been a very strange, scary night, and we knew that there would never be another one like it.

6. First, let me tell you about the scariest dream I ever had.

7. Afterward, the mean, old troll never crossed that bridge again.

8. Next we pulled out our hammers and stakes and began putting up our tents.

9. As a result, the little, old dog never went hungry again.

10. Today is going to be the best day of my life!

11. Finally, the big, bad wolf ran away.

12. Meanwhile, the hairy, little monster waited for just the right moment.

Build a Sentence

Tell about . . . .

Somebody   doing   something.

Half Sentences

1. The round little pig _____.

2. _____ was driving the new car.

3. _____ was catching a slimy fish.

4. The big black bear was _____.

5. _____ is swimming in the water.

6. _____ flies high in the sky.

7. The giant monster _____.

8. _____ flew on a broomstick.

9. The yellow bus _____.

10. _____ went to sleep.

11. The funny clown _____.

12. _____ jumped over the fence.

13. _____ was hiding under the bed.

14. The tiny baby mouse _____.

"Who" Picture Cards

boy

girl

man

woman

bear

monkey

Teaching Beginning Writing © 1999 Creative Teaching Press

"Who" Picture Cards

lion

spider

cat

dog

snake

clown

"Who" Picture Cards

cowboy

doctor

king

queen

$\begin{array}{r} 3 \\ +\ 3 \\ \hline \end{array}$

teacher

monster

"Who" Picture Cards

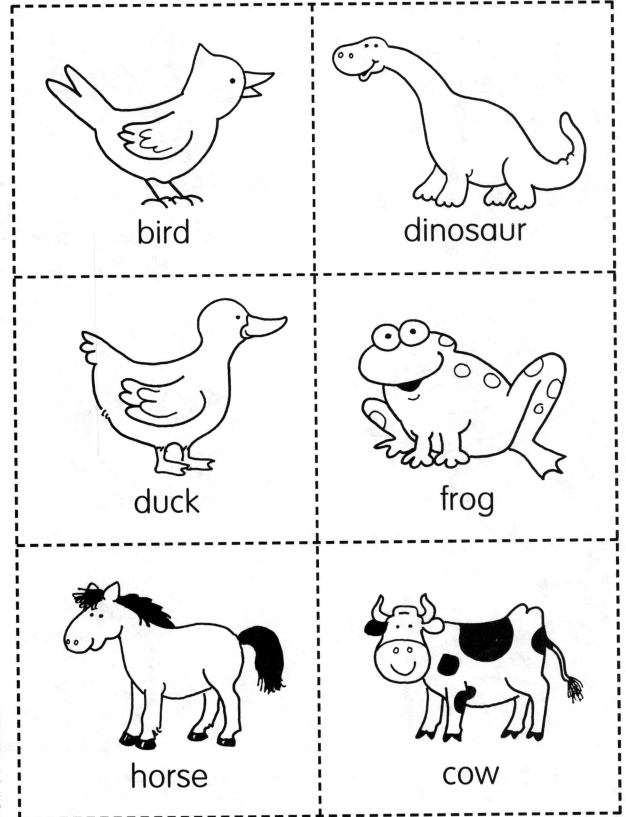

bird

dinosaur

duck

frog

horse

cow

"Doing What" Picture Cards

stands

dances

flies

swings

hides

jumps

"Doing What" Picture Cards

swims

runs

sings

walks

eats

drinks

"Doing What" Picture Cards

climbs

rides

digs

sleeps

sees

hears

"Doing What" Picture Cards

writes

draws

sits

finds

crawls

cries

"Where" Picture Cards

circus

tree

castle

pond

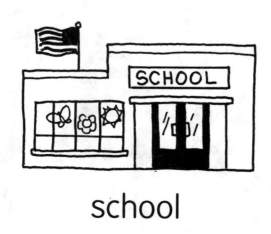

school

classroom

Teaching Beginning Writing © 1999 Creative Teaching Press

"Where" Picture Cards

store

zoo

airplane

park

garden

sky

Teaching Beginning Writing © 1999 Creative Teaching Press

"Where" Picture Cards

hole

forest

house

bedroom

kitchen

hill

Sample Picture-Card Sentences

A frog jumps into the pond.   (frog, jumps, pond)

The boy hides behind a tree.   (boy, hides, tree)

The teacher walks into the classroom.   (teacher, walks, classroom)

The dog digs a hole.   (dog, digs, hole)

A spider crawls in the garden.   (spider, crawls, garden)

The girl dances in her bedroom.   (girl, dances, bedroom)

A king finds the castle.   (king, finds, castle)

The bear sleeps in the forest.   (bear, sleeps, forest)

A bird flies high in the sky.   (bird, flies, sky)

The man runs up a hill.   (man, runs, hill)

A monkey swings on a tree.   (monkey, swings, tree)

The duck swims in a pond.   (duck, swims, pond)

The woman walks to the store.   (woman, walks, store)

Flip-Open Fun

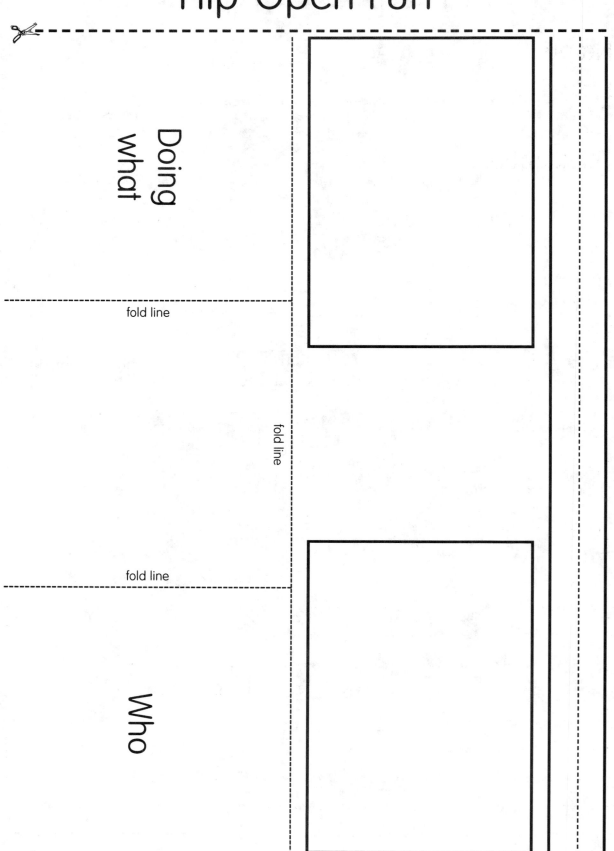

Doing
what

fold line

fold line

Who

Teaching Beginning Writing © 1999 Creative Teaching Press

Imagination Time

Name _____

Date _____

Think about it.

Who?   Doing what?   Where?

Draw it on another sheet of paper.

Write about it.
_____
- -
_____
- -
_____
- -
_____
- -
_____
- -
_____
- -
_____

Teaching Beginning Writing © 1999 Creative Teaching Press

Filmstrip Pattern

Staple blank paper strips here.

A

Cut the slits.

B

Teaching Beginning Writing © 1999 Creative Teaching Press

Cinquains

Ghosts

White, scary

Flying, booing, disappearing

Come on Halloween

Ghosts

School

Fun, friendly

Learning, sharing, playing

A happy place to be

School

Santa

Jolly, fat

Giving, sharing, surprising

Brings happiness to children

Santa

How to write a personal cinquain:

1. Your name

2. How you look and feel

3. Three things you're good at

4. Makes _____(fill in the blank)

5. Your name

Example:

Ryan

Handsome, happy

Wrestling, running, drawing

Makes people laugh

Ryan

Questions and Answers

Name _____

Date _____

DIRECTIONS: Fill in the blanks to complete each sentence. When you are finished, read the story you have just written! Then draw a picture on another sheet of paper to go along with your story.

I have a _____

It is _____

and _____

It can _____

but it can't _____

I like _____

because _____

Mr. Story Face

Story Frames

Once upon a time I saw _____.

He looked _____ and _____.

He had _____ and _____.

He liked to _____

because _____.

- -

You should have seen _____.

She looked so _____ because _____

_____.

She wanted to _____

_____.

But instead she _____.

- -

If I had my very own _____

I would _____.

Then I would _____

because _____

Teaching Beginning Writing © 1999 Creative Teaching Press

Story Frames

Once upon a time I wandered into a scary _____.

It was _____. It looked so _____

_____. I was afraid because _____

_____.

- -

Once there was a _____ named _____.

She had lots of _____ and a funny _____

_____. She looked _____.

She surprised everyone when _____.

- -

One dark night I made a wish on a _____ star. I wished that _____

_____. That would be

really fun because _____.

If I had a second wish, it would be _____.

I like wishes, especially when they come true!

Teaching Beginning Writing © 1999 Creative Teaching Press

Story Frames

Once there was a _____ and a _____.

They were best friends. They lived _____ where it was

_____. When it was sunny they liked to

_____ in the _____.

When it snowed they liked to _____ on the

_____. They had fun together because _____

_____.

- -

On _____, I went to _____ party. It was

for my friend _____. He was going to be _____ years

old. He got lots of presents like _____ and

_____. He liked _____ the best

because _____.

- -

There was a little fish named _____.

She loved to _____ and _____.

One day she saw a big, scary _____. She had to get away.

She _____.

Then she _____.

Teaching Beginning Writing © 1999 Creative Teaching Press

Stretch It!

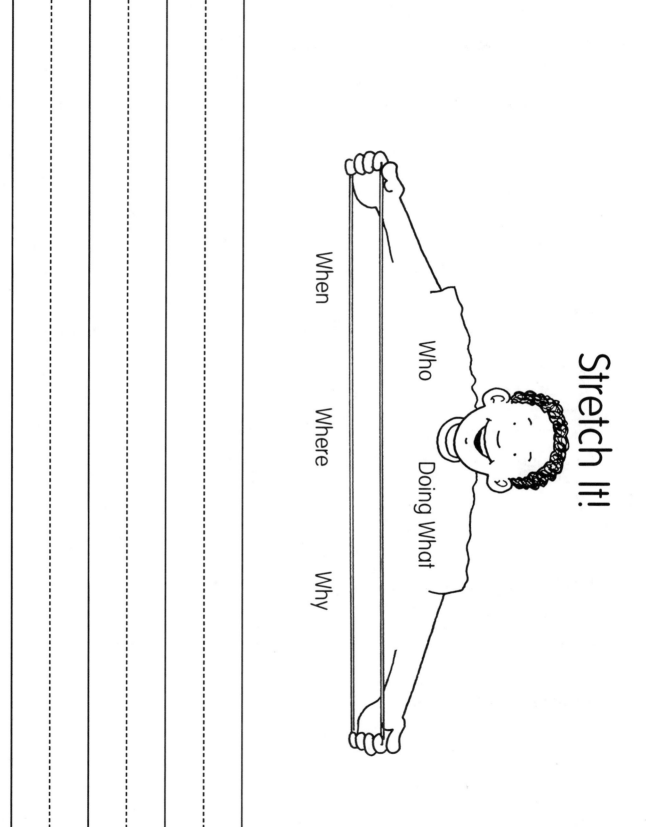

Who   Doing What

When   Where   Why

Peek-a-Boo Story

5 Why

2 Where

fold line

4 Doing what

fold line

3 Who

1 When

Teaching Beginning Writing © 1999 Creative Teaching Press

Connect a Story

Name _____

Date _____

Read My Mind

Three words that describe it:

What can it do?

Where is it?

When did you get it?

Use all this information to write one complete sentence.

Sentence Builder

When	Who	Is Doing What	Where	Why

Story Ladders

Short Story Ladder

Finally

Next

Then

First

Once . . .

- -

Super Story Ladder

Finally

Next

Then

First

Once . . .

Story Walk

Story Stumpers

1. Where did the story take place (the setting)?

2. Who was the main character?

3. Which describing words were used in the story to tell how the character looked?

4. What word was used that is the opposite of _____?

5. What is a two-syllable word that was used in the story?

6. Think of a word that was used that means the same as _____?

7. When did the story take place?

8. What did the main character do in the story?

9. Which "doing" words (verbs) were used in the story?

10. How did the main character feel?

11. Why did the character feel that way?

12. Which compound words were used in the story?

13. Which words in the story began with the sound _____.

14. What happened in the middle of the story?

15. What happened at the end of the story?

Teaching Beginning Writing © 1999 Creative Teaching Press

Dinosaur Details

Digging for Details

Name _____

Date _____

Teaching Beginning Writing © 1999 Creative Teaching Press

Super Story Walk

My Best Friend

I think that I am the luckiest person alive because I have Shag. You can tell from his name that my dog is a little fur ball. He has white, shaggy hair from head to toe, and when he lies on the floor, he looks just like a rug. It didn't take me long to teach him tricks because he is so smart. I taught Shag how to fetch. Now he can get the morning newspaper from the porch. He even gets his dish when it is time for me to feed him! I take good care of Shag because I love him so much. We play together every day, and he sleeps with me every night. Shag even kisses me good night! He makes me feel special. I am so lucky to have Shag. He is the best dog in the whole world!

Story Snake

Somebody

Somewhere

Something

So then . . . . .

Super Writer

Awarded to _____

for writing complete, detailed sentences
that have a beginning, a middle, and an end.

Signed _____

Date _____

Beginning middle end

- -

Writing Wiz!

Awarded to

_____

for writing descriptive,
vivid stories that "come to life."

Signed _____

Date _____